◀ (Front endpaper) Stilt fishermen near a coastal village outside Thái Bình City
▶ Open-fire cooking at a village street kitchen

Vietnamese
food and food culture

Paul B. Kennedy

TUTTLE Publishing
Tokyo | Rutland, Vermont | Singapore

◀ **Lunch aboard a day cruise in Hạ Long Bay**
▼ **Vendors setting up a fish market on the beach**

To appreciate the culture, you must understand the food.
To appreciate the food, you must understand the culture.

—PAUL B. KENNEDY

Contents

Main Dishes

Drinks and Desserts

▲ **(Left) The rice fields in Mai Châu**
(Right) A worker sorting pineapples in Hanoi
◄ **(Left) Chicken, pork and beef bánh mì sandwiches with veggies and herbs**
(Right) Limes for sale at a Vietnamese market

A day of traveling will bring a basket full of learning.

—VIETNAMESE PROVERB

Travel Makes the Hungry Satisfied

Before we begin, I want to explain what I mean when I use the word "travel." There are those who vacation, and then there are those who travel. Vacationers take a break from everyday life. During their temporary escape, they wear blinders—their main goal is to relax in new surroundings. Travelers, on the other hand, are curious. They're hungry to learn and absorb details, and they use trips to whet their curiosity.

To satisfy my own curiosity, when I leave home, I go on my own. Traveling with friends prevents me from receiving what every moment may offer. Fellow travelers divert my attention from my surroundings. But traveling alone is a crash course in empathy. It provides understanding and compassion that's impossible to achieve any other way. It can help the shy become confident, the lonely feel included, and the quiet be heard. Traveling solo also provides the perfect climate for understanding and appreciating the local cuisine with a clear mind and no distractions.

Though food is my profession and passion, I never thought I'd write a cookbook. It wasn't an easy task, and there were times I wished I hadn't begun! But I believe we are all responsible for sharing our experiences to improve the common good, and cookbooks can be an enormous catalyst for learning and change. But first, I had to find my voice and my platform.

The process led me to fully engage with and understand the value of the relationship between what we eat, how we prepare a meal, and culture. And creating *Vietnamese Food and Food Culture* reinforced the critical importance of travel to my work.

Learning about a new place means learning about the people who have created the culture. I've written this book to introduce you to authentic Vietnamese cooking and to the people who crafted this cuisine. I've also written this from the point of view of an ex-pat, a traveler, a chef and a teacher in Vietnam. These recipes provide opportunities to experience something new and different. If you let them, they can begin to expand your perspective of the world. And, although they provide measurements, they are really just outlines. Receive these recipes as stories and then make each of them your own.

I hope you will engage with this glimpse of the Vietnamese way of life and be as drawn to the country as I am. And, if you are able to travel abroad, I hope you'll travel here. To

◀ **(Clockwise from top right) Sightseeing in Hội An; Water buffalo fodder delivery on Phú Quốc Island; A Hanoi street corner; Fish at the pier on Lý Sơn Island; Hội An locals enjoying street food;** *Bánh xèo—* **sizzling pancakes**

9

not experience Vietnam first-hand would be to shortchange yourself.

When we're born, our lives are a book with blank pages. What each chapter contains is up to us. We grow by forcing ourselves to step outside of our comfort zones—whether trying new recipes or choosing to travel alone. If you decide to embrace both, you'll open your mind and shape your values.

I hope that you will enjoy this book for what it is: a collection of delicious recipes, colorful photographs and tidbits about Vietnamese culture arranged in a light-hearted way. *Vietnamese Food and Food Culture* is neither a 30-minute-meal cookbook nor a history book on Vietnam. It's an invitation to travel to Vietnam yourself and join me for a bowl of phở.

Travel introduces exotic foods

In Vietnam, you'll eat the best pineapple you'll ever taste in your life, or, if you're feeling adventurous, you might try Nước Yến, a drink made from bird saliva and white fungus! Further broaden your palate with fertilized duck eggs, chicken feet or a silk worm dish! Wash it all down with a bottle of rambutan juice, which will only cost you twenty cents when purchased by the roadside.

Travel brings color to life

Trucks are commonly bronze; government buildings yellow; the garbage collectors wear pastels. There is a city where almost every building is the same tone and shade of yellow. If you find yourself in these surroundings, you must be in Hội An. Throughout the country and in

general, the ceiling fans are turquoise, oscillating fans, orange. Bright yellow bamboo coracle boats—you'll see them everywhere—were once used only for fishing because they're lightweight and difficult to overturn. One-armed rowing takes some practice, but it's a great way for you to see Vietnam from the water.

Travel makes the distracted aware

◀ (Top) Lan Ha Bay; (Bottom) Locals at the weekend market in Sapa ▼ Bùi Viện "beer street" in Ho Chi Minh City

Everyone has an altar for praying, even though the majority of the population isn't religious; traditions and rituals are more widely followed than belief. In addition to the day a person is born, everyone shares another birthday on the first day of the lunar calendar. Weddings last for days and can include female representatives from most families in a neighborhood.

Travel puts life into perspective

As with weddings, funerals are also communal displays. Families pay for extra mourners to attend, demonstrating that the deceased was well-liked. In parts of Vietnam, when loved ones pass away, they are temporarily buried for a period of three years. Afterward, the bones are moved to a permanent burial location.

Because land—specifically, land appropriate for burial plots—is so expensive and the remains will be moved later anyway, many choose to temporarily bury their dead in rice paddies. The fish that swim about in the paddies are more than happy to help clean the bones. The fish of Ninh Binh, the town where I first learned of this practice, were, curiously,

the most delicious I've ever eaten. As the Vietnamese say, "Life is a temporary stop, death is the journey home."

Travel gives you insight on the lives of others

Teachers are underpaid in Vietnam; most make $250 US dollars a month, around minimum wage. Street vendors make $130 US a month, so don't offer them less money than they request. Quitting before Tet is a common problem because employees want time off around the holiday. Being a police officer carries prestige and becoming one often requires having connections or an exchange of money. Police "fine" drunk drivers by making them do push-ups on the side of the road. Here, people don't stay home for "snow days," but they do for heavy "rain days."

▶ (Clockwise from top left) Balancing act with some *bánh rán* on Bùi Viện Street in Ho Chi Minh City; Pineapples for sale in a Mekong Delta floating market; Preparing spring rolls in a market ▼ A diner enjoys a bowl of *bún chả* in Hanoi

Travel makes you appreciate the value of a dollar

For $35 you can buy a one-way airline ticket across the country. In US dollars, it costs $4 to have a tech come to your house to replace the toner on your printer. Teeth cleaning and x-rays cost $8 total for both, or you can get a $3 haircut and shave. Want a pet? Miniature pinschers go for $22. Ballpoint pens cost 13 cents each. A car wash is $2.20, but a motorbike wash is only 88 cents. For $2.40, you could buy a loaf of bread and a dozen duck eggs, but lobster, at this moment, costs $45 a pound. All you can eat at a restaurant will run you between $6.62 and $15.45 per person.

Travel gives you a fresh perspective on food and faith

In Vietnam, fresh coconut water costs only $1.33 a quart. But some once valued coconuts to a different degree altogether: A religion—or shall we call it a cult, the "Coconut Religion," was established in Vietnam. It was founded in 1963 by Vietnamese mystic Nguyễn Thành Nam ("the Coconut Monk"). Its practice called for consuming only coconut meat and drinking only coconut milk. Author John Steinbeck's son, John Steinbeck IV, was a devotee. Today, the cult has been outlawed, but the dilapidated commune still exists on Phoenix Island in the Mekong Delta.

Travel makes the bored curious

Many think that durian smells like a rotten animal and tastes like onions saturated with turpentine, but somehow, it's still one of the most popular fruits in Vietnam—and, of course, widely eaten throughout Asia. Restaurants may provide diners with plastic gloves so the smell won't permeate the skin! Despite it all, people manage to eat durian without vomiting. If you've tried it and your experience doesn't match that description, then the fruit wasn't ripe! For many, rat meat is an acquired taste. Although you'll find them served more commonly in homes than in restaurants, the demand for this food is high enough that a cross-border rat trade has been established with neighboring Cambodia. ◼

◀ **(Top) Woman selling fruits in a floating market in the Mekong Delta (Bottom) A bowl of phở served in Ho Chi Minh City ▼ Fishing at sunrise in Phú Yên Province**

Vietnamese Essentials

As I developed this book, I experienced first-hand how complex some of these recipes are to prepare. I simplified, when possible, but only if that process respected the spirit of the food. Yet I know some steps are labor-intensive. So, I've balanced the complicated with more straightforward recipes. Even so, you might not be familiar with all of the ingredients. I hope this is the case because that's the best way to learn! You'll find many elements you'll need at most Asian markets. If not, you should be able to track them down online.

Vietnamese dishes are generally light on protein and heavy on greens and herbs. Cooks often add sugar to foods we eat unsweetened in the States. But in Vietnam, you will always find assorted layers of unique and complementary flavors and spices. It's uncommon to find authentic ethnic dishes outside of the country or region from which they originate. For example, the phở of the north is more austere and sophisticated than that of the south, so it's understandable that interpretations of it 9,000 miles away in the United States would be completely different, as well.

◀ **Street market vendor in Hanoi with eggplant, peppers, cabbage and other local fruits and vegetables**

The food here reflects the nation's long and colorful history, tropical climate, and distinct geography. It's the truest farm-to-table experience you could hope to experience—you won't find avocados imported from Mexico or frozen octopus flown in from Portugal. The Vietnamese use ingredients that are grown, fished, or raised locally. How local? Foods rarely come from more than a short drive away.

I often use the term "season to taste" or "season as needed." Each of our palates is unique and reflects salt sensitivities or variations in our olfactory receptor genes that make us perceive foods differently. Our tastes for seasonings do indeed vary—and much of that variation is simply a matter of individual preference. And too, consider the abundant natural differences in the taste and aromas of ingredients—for example, some peppers are hotter than others, even if the come from the same plant.

I also want to mention storage and harvesting issues. Cinnamon harvested in Sri Lanka that is processed and stored for years before finding its way into your pantry will have a completely different flavor and color than fresh cinnamon my neighbors might purchase at local markets, wherever they live in Vietnam. That's just the way Mother Nature (and our supply chain) works. Accept it. Embrace it.

None of this matters if you consider recipes to be learning tools. Recipes should never stress you out. If you try something and it doesn't turn out the first time, please don't perceive that as a failure. Recipes serve to help you better understand ingredients and appreciate a culture. I hope these recipes challenge you. I hope they make you curious. I hope they inspire you.

Sauces, Pastes, Oil and Vinegar

Fermented shrimp paste joins fish sauce and soy sauce to form the "holy trinity" of ingredients in Vietnamese cuisine. They all provide character and complexity, so be sure you never leave them out—especially the shrimp paste!

Anchovy sauce: Similar to fish sauce but cured differently, this fermented sauce features a much stronger aroma and a more pungent flavor.

Annatto oil: This oil, a deep shade of red, adds color and an earthy, peppery flavor to any dish. To make it, a base vegetable oil is infused with annatto seeds, which come from the achiote tree.

Chili paste: This thick, versatile paste is made of ground chili peppers, oil, vinegar and salt.

Chili pastes are available in different levels of spiciness.

Fermented shrimp paste: Shrimp paste, which is made with ground-up shrimp, has a very strong flavor and a pungent smell. It's an acquired taste, but this condiment is an important ingredient in many Asian recipes and shouldn't be substituted for or omitted.

Fish sauce: This essential ingredient is salty and savory; always select an aged fish sauce for the best flavor. A little fish sauce goes a long way.

Oyster sauce: This dark, syrupy sauce with a sweet, savory and salty flavor is made with oyster juice, salt, sugar and (typically) cornstarch.

Anchovy sauce

Chili paste

Annatto oil

Fermented shrimp paste

Pandan extract ("paste"): This concentrate has a naturally sweet and very distinctive grassy vanilla flavor. To make it, leaves from the pandan plant are ground up and the fibrous pieces are removed.

Rice wine vinegar: Made from fermented rice, this vinegar (also known as rice vinegar) is both slightly sweet and sour.

Soy sauce: A sauce made from fermented soybean paste that provides a salty umami flavor. It's available in many types, including regular, low sodium, flavored, dark and thick. Dark soy sauce is sweeter and richer, with a consistency like molasses. Thick soy sauce is both darker and sweeter than dark sauce; it has a paste-like consistency.

Sweet chili sauce: This tangy and spicy sauce with a sweet flavor profile is made from dried chili peppers, vinegar, sugar, garlic and fish sauce.

Tamarind paste: Made from the tamarind fruit, this thick pulp delivers sweet and sour flavors to Asian dishes.

Tamarind sauce: Made from the pulp of the tamarind fruit, this sauce can be found in a variety of thicknesses, but it is always smooth and features a sweet yet tart flavor profile.

Sugars and Spices

Cane sugar: Cane sugar is made exclusively from the tropical sugar cane plant and has a more intense flavor than granulated sugars made from sugar beets.

Fish sauce

Pandan extract ("paste")

Rice wine vinegar

Oyster sauce

Soy sauce

Curry powder

Sweet chili sauce

Five spice powder

Galangal

Tamarind paste

Palm sugar

Tamarind sauce

22

Curry powder: This powder is a mixture of turmeric, ginger, cumin, black pepper and sometimes cinnamon. Although Indian in origin, it's used in all types of Asian cooking.

Five spice powder: Also known as Chinese five spice, this spice blend is made of cinnamon, fennel, star anise, cloves and Szechuan pepper. Its flavor is sweet and warm, with a licorice note thanks to the star anise.

Galangal: Related to both ginger and turmeric, this underrated spice has a strong, sharp smell but imparts a clean and citrusy flavor with a hint of pine.

Palm sugar: Made from date palm or sugar palm, this type of sugar is light brown in color and has a mild caramel flavor.

Shrimp powder: This powder, made of dried, ground shrimp, is a natural flavor enhancer with a deeply salty and fishy taste.

Star anise: A key ingredient in Asian cooking, star anise is a spice that comes from the fruit of the Chinese evergreen tree; it has a flavor and fragrance that is similar to licorice.

Sugar: The most commonly found multi-purpose sugar for cooking is granulated and refined white table sugar, which is made from either sugar beets or sugar cane.

Turmeric powder: Part of the ginger family, turmeric adds a lovely yellow hue and an earthy, somewhat bitter flavor to dishes.

Shrimp powder

Star anise

Turmeric powder

23

Betel leaves

Lemongrass

Perilla leaves

Bird's eye chili peppers

Vietnamese basil

Culantro

24

Fresh Herbs

Betel leaves: These heart-shaped leaves, which are indigenous to Asia, have a peppery flavor with a slight degree of bitterness.

Bird's eye chili peppers: Also known as Thai chili peppers, they are used extensively in Asian cooking. Small, slender and bright red, the peppers vary in terms of heat. It's not recommended to substitute these with other peppers.

Coriander: This herb, which is a member of the parsley family, provides a distinctive pungent and citrusy flavor to dishes. Both the leaves and stems are edible; it is also known as cilantro.

Culantro: This herb, which has sawtooth-edged leaves, has a similar aroma and flavor to coriander leaves (cilantro), but is much stronger.

Lemongrass: This tropical grass is native to southeast Asia and has a lemony aroma and a citrus flavor.

Perilla leaves: This very popular Asian herb imparts a grassy flavor with subtle notes of licorice. The herb is often used in cooking and in craft cocktails. The leaves are sold fresh, frozen or dried.

Thai basil: A member of the basil family, Thai basil has purple stems and flowers with green leaves, a clove aroma and an anise-like flavor.

Vietnamese basil: This type of basil is similar to Thai basil but has slightly smaller leaves. It is often substituted for, and confused with, Thai basil.

Coriander

Thai basil

Vietnamese mint

Coconut soda

Coconut milk

Coconut pieces

Broken rice

26

Vietnamese mint: Also known as Vietnamese coriander, this herb has a minty, peppery flavor.

Coconut

Coconut cream: This thick cream is made from coconut milk. Do not confuse it with "cream of coconut," which is a sweetened blend of coconut meat, water and sugar.

Coconut milk: Coconut milk is a milky-white liquid naturally extracted from the grated flesh of mature brown coconuts, with little or no water added. Young green coconuts are typically harvested for coconut water.

Coconut pieces: These chunks or pieces of coconut flesh are consumed fresh or dried.

Coconut soda: This fizzy coconut-flavored drink is sweetened with sugar or high-fructose corn syrup.

Rice

Broken rice: Traditionally a food for the poor, because broken pieces of rice were not considered salable.

Rice paper wrappers: Also known as rice paper sheets, these super-thin wrappers are usually made of rice, water and salt. Some are made from a blend of rice flour and tapioca flour.

Sticky rice: Also known as "glutinous rice" or "sweet rice." This grain, which is mainly found in Asia, has a very low amylose content and a high amount of amylopectin, which causes it to become sticky when cooked.

White rice: White rice is milled, and the husk, bran and germ are removed.

Rice paper wrappers

White rice

Sticky rice

Agave nectar

Banana leaves

Banana flowers

Chicken fat

Dried shiitake mushrooms

Dried wood ear mushrooms

Other Ingredients

Agave nectar: This syrup, a natural sweetener, is derived from the blue agave plant.

Banana flowers: Also known as "banana blossoms," these flowers are usually sold dried or frozen and whole or thinly sliced. They have a very subtle flavor but a delicate banana aroma, especially when they are fresh.

Banana leaves: These waterproof leaves are commonly used in Asian cooking for steaming. When foods are steamed in the leaves, they impart a very distinct, yet subtle, sweetness.

Chicken fat: In some cultures known as "schmaltz," this rendered fat is used in lieu of butter or oil to impart rich, savory flavor.

Cornstarch: This corn-derived starch is also known as "corn flour."

Dried shiitake mushrooms: These dried mushrooms have a meaty, smoky flavor and a pungent smell prior to cooking.

Dried wood ear mushrooms: Also known as "wood fungus mushrooms," these have a mild and earthy flavor but very little fragrance. After they are cooked, they take on a gelatinous and crunchy texture.

Grapefruit extract: This extract is made from grapefruit seeds, pulp and membranes. It adds a tangy citrus flavor to recipes.

Longan: This fruit, a relative of the lychee, has a tough, brown shell and sweet, white flesh.

Lotus seeds: Available fresh, dried or canned, the seeds of the lotus plant can be eaten raw or cooked. They provide a mild, nutty and slightly sweet flavor.

Longan

Lotus seeds

Lychee: The scaly skin of the fruit of the lychee tree is a reddish pink color. Its pulp is sweet and juicy, and each fruit has a single large seed.

Mayonnaise: Vietnamese mayonnaise is smoother, richer, fattier and yellower than popular commercial brands in the United States.

Mung beans: A member of the legume family, also known as *maash* or "green gram," these beans are extremely versatile and used in sweet and savory dishes alike. While they look like regular garden beans, they possess a slightly sweet and nutty flavor.

Quail eggs: Similar in flavor to duck eggs, quail eggs are smaller in size, creamier, and have a higher yolk-to-white ratio.

Shrimp flakes: Dried shrimp flakes are fluffy and have a delicious briny flavor.

Tofu (firm): Also known as bean curd, tofu has very little inherent flavor. It is created by curdling soy milk into solid blocks. Firm tofu, the densest type, contains the least moisture, as most of the water is pressed out of it.

Quail eggs

Mung beans

Lychee

Dipping Sauce
Nước Chấm

1 tablespoon sugar
1 tablespoon fish sauce
2 teaspoons rice wine vinegar
2 teaspoons fresh lime juice
3 cloves garlic, finely chopped
⅓ cup (80 ml) water
1 bird's eye chili pepper, seeded and finely chopped

This mildly spicy, slightly sweet and sour condiment is superb on grilled meats, and will liven up any hand-held street food.

1 In a small mixing bowl, whisk together the sugar, fish sauce, rice vinegar, lime juice, garlic, water and chili pepper until the sugar is dissolved.

Green Onion Oil
Mỡ Hành

¼ cup (60 ml) vegetable oil
¼ teaspoon fine sea salt
½ cup (25 g) thinly sliced green onions (scallions), green parts

This simple and delicious vibrant green garnish is traditionally brushed or drizzled over grilled meats and vegetables, rice and rice noodle dishes.

1 Heat the oil and salt in a small saucepan over medium heat. Add the green onion and stir for 10 seconds. Remove from the heat and transfer to another container. Refrigerate for 20 minutes to help the green onion slices keep their color. Once cool, let sit at room temperature until ready to serve.

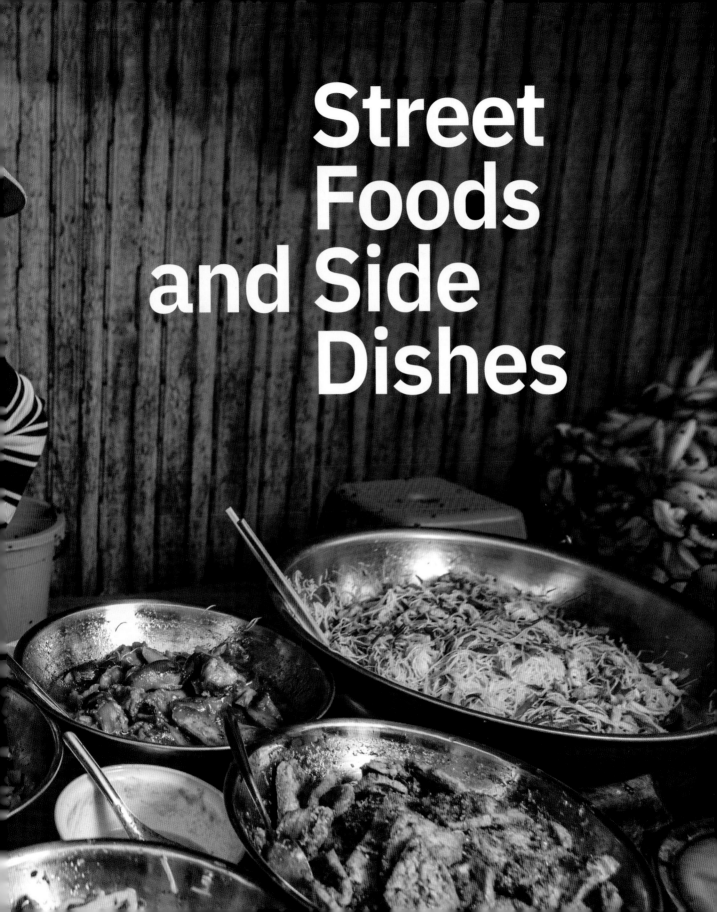

Street Foods and Side Dishes

Street Foods and Side Dishes

Travel broadens your palate

In Vietnam, milk and spaghetti are both unusually sweet. Mayonnaise comes in pouches. When you purchase a drink on the street, it'll likely be served in a lightly rinsed used plastic water bottle. Fruit is eaten with salt while still unripe and bitter. The meat is chewy, no two apples taste the same, and every fifth cucumber is so bitter it's inedible. Gum chewing is rare, but dried squid tastes like lobster flavored chewing gum.

Travel can be familiar too

Looking for something more familiar? Sunflowers are grown in Vietnam as fodder, but the seeds are so abundant that they're served with virtually every beverage at restaurants and passed around like hors d'oeuvres at weddings. Vietnam is the leader in cashew production, but the nuts (which are actually seeds) are too expensive for most locals, so the majority of crop is exported. The "cashew apple" is a byproduct that is consumed as fresh fruit or fermented into wine.

Travel makes you appreciate the comforts of home

In Vietnam, when you lean against a streetlamp, prepare for a shock, because wiring is typically not grounded. Most Vietnamese homes don't have ovens or stoves; instead, they have portable stovetops. Hardly anyone owns a bathroom scale. Freezers are full of food stored in grocery-style plastic bags, not storage containers.

◄ Cooking traditional *bánh xèo* pancakes at a restaurant in An Giang, Mekong Delta

Travel brings new remedies

The Vietnamese believe that eating the sweet, milky pulp of a custard apple can cure a fever. Another curative, *khổ qua* (bitter melon), is a wart-covered gourd used for both culinary and medicinal purposes. Its curative properties are said to include cancer prevention, and it is used to treat ulcers, malaria, skin disorders, inflammation and other maladies.

Travel makes the lost found

Addresses in Vietnam often include a string of street names leading to a destination from the main street, to one lane, to another. Crossing streets is a thrilling challenge—the roads are crammed with motorbikes. If you're brave enough to just keep walking, the bikers will avoid you.

Travel reveals curious customs

You won't see locals at the beach during the day because most residents shun suntans. Shopping malls are full at Christmas, but people gather to browse, not buy. Bad luck is said to come your way if you decide to clean during the Tet holiday.

Travel brings new outfits to try

Traditional garb throughout the year includes *áo dài*, a long, tight-fitting silk top with slits on the sides and matching pants. *Áo bà ba*, a traditional southern Vietnamese garment, consists of long-sleeved pajama-style outfits of silk. How wonderful it is get away with wearing pajamas in public! Throughout the country, students dress tracksuit uniforms; many are blue and white.

Makes 6–8 Spring Rolls
Prep time: 25 mins
Cook time: 5–10 mins

For the peanut sauce:
½ cup (135 g) creamy
    peanut butter
2 teaspoons honey
2 teaspoons low sodium
    soy sauce
2 teaspoons rice wine
    vinegar
2 cloves garlic, minced
One 1-in (2.5-cm) piece
    fresh ginger, peeled
    and grated
1 teaspoon toasted
    sesame oil
1 teaspoon fresh lime juice
Water, as needed
1 carrot, cut into thin
    matchsticks (optional)

For the spring rolls:
2 oz (50 g) dried rice
    noodles (vermicelli)
⅓ cup (15 g) thinly sliced
    green onions (scallions)
⅓ cup (10 g) coarsely
    chopped coriander
    leaves (cilantro)
⅓ cup (10 g) coarsely
    chopped mint
1 carrot, cut into thin
    matchsticks
2 cucumbers, cut into thin
    matchsticks
12–16 rice paper wrappers
2 cups (40 g) mixed greens
2 cups (210 g) bean sprouts
8 oz (250 g) extra jumbo
    shrimp (16/20), cooked,
    peeled, and deveined

Fresh Shrimp Spring Rolls

Nem Cuốn

I've made these spring rolls often during my time in Hanoi—always in the company of a wonderful group of local friends. Connecting with others and exchanging stories about yourself over food are among my favorite things to do, and spring rolls are the perfect dish to share around a table.

1 For the peanut sauce: In a medium mixing bowl, whisk together the peanut butter, honey, soy sauce, rice vinegar, garlic, ginger, sesame oil and lime juice until mixed thoroughly. Add water, if needed, to achieve the desired consistency: smooth, creamy, and free of lumps. Transfer the sauce to a serving bowl and garnish with carrot, if using.

2 For the spring rolls: Prepare the rice noodles according to the package instructions, rinse with cold water, and set aside. In a small bowl, combine the green onion, coriander leaves and mint. In a separate bowl, combine the carrot and cucumber.

3 Fill a shallow bowl with warm water. Stack two rice paper sheets and submerge them in the water for a few seconds until pliable. Carefully lay them onto a flat surface. Evenly distributing the ingredients, add a portion of the herbs along the bottom edge of thew rice papers, leaving about 1 inch (2.5 cm) of rice paper on either side of the filling. Top the herbs with the noodles, mixed greens, sprouts, carrot, cucumber and whole shrimp. Roll the sheet away from you halfway, holding the ingredients compactly inside the wrapper. Next, fold the 1-inch (2.5-cm) sides inward over the filling and continue rolling until the spring roll is wrapped firmly. Repeat with the remaining wrappers and ingredients. Serve the spring rolls with peanut sauce on the side for dipping.

Grilled Corn on the Cob

Ngô Nướng

Makes 6 Servings
Prep time: 10 mins
Cook time: 10 mins

¼ cup (60 g) unsalted butter
1 teaspoon brown sugar
1 teaspoon white pepper
2 teaspoons fish sauce
6 green onions (scallions), green parts only, thinly sliced
6 ears sweet summer corn, husked
Vegetable oil, for brushing
Zest of 1 lime (optional)

Although this recipe calls for sweet summer corn, on the streets of Vietnam, this dish often substitutes glutinous, or waxy, corn instead. Glutinous corn is a very starchy type that's often used to feed livestock. It's... well, it's chewy, which is why I suggest sweet summer corn instead.

1 In a small saucepan, melt the butter over medium heat. Add the brown sugar and white pepper and mix until the sugar is dissolved. Add the fish sauce and green onion, lower the heat to medium-low, and allow to simmer, stirring frequently, until the sauce begins to thicken.

2 Preheat a grill to high heat. Slather the corn with the green onion butter and grill, uncovered. Turn the corn every 2–3 minutes while continuing to baste, until the kernels are tender and charred. Remove from the grill and drizzle with the remaining green onion butter. Sprinkle with lime zest, if using, and serve warm.

Steamed Rice Cakes with Dried Shrimp

Bánh Bèo Tôm Cháy

Makes 8 Servings
Prep time: 1 hour
Cook time: 30–40 mins

Green Onion Oil (see page 31)

For the batter:
2 cups (280 g) rice flour
¼ cup (30 g) tapioca flour
1 teaspoon salt
½ teaspoon turmeric
4 cups (1 liter) warm water

For the toppings:
½ cup (100 g) dried split mung beans, soaked overnight and drained
1 teaspoon salt
1 teaspoon sugar
¼ teaspoon ground white pepper
8 oz (250 g) skinless pork belly, cut into ½-in (1.25-cm) cubes
1 clove garlic, minced
4 teaspoons sliced green onions (scallions)
½ cup (20 g) dried shrimp, soaked in water for 1 hour
Vegetable oil, as needed

If a restaurant only has one dish on its menu, it's likely that it's a dish you must try. That's how I discovered the wonderful rice cakes featured in this recipe—what good fortune! Besides simply being tasty, these cakes are great for breakfast, lunch or a terrific midday snack. Silver dollar in size, these are named for the water lilies found throughout Huế, a town in central Vietnam. The recipe was originally developed in the Nguyễn dynasty for an emperor who requested a unique dish that his 104 wives would enjoy. Today, they're a quintessential Huế snack.

1 Prepare the Green Onion Oil.

2 For the batter: Sift the rice flour, tapioca flour, salt and turmeric together into a bowl. Add the water and whisk until there are no lumps. Set aside to rest for 1 hour.

3 Meanwhile, steam the mung beans in a large pot in 1 inch (2.5 cm) of water over medium-high heat for 15 minutes or until soft. Add the mung beans, salt, sugar and white pepper to a food processor and process until smooth. Transfer the mung bean paste to a bowl and clean out the food processor.

4 Fry the pork belly in a preheated skillet set over medium-high heat for about 7–10 minutes, or until crispy. Add the garlic and green onion and cook for another minute. Reserve 2 tablespoons of the fat and transfer the pork to a plate lined with paper towels.

5 Drain the soaked shrimp and pat dry with paper towels to remove excess moisture. Pulse the shrimp in the food processor until finely ground. Heat the reserved 2 tablespoons of pork fat in the skillet over medium heat. Add the shrimp and cook, stirring frequently, until the mixture loses moisture and the texture starts to become floss-like, about 5 minutes. Set aside.

6 Select either a miniature muffin pan or small bowls (ideally about 2 × 1 inch / 5 × 2.5 cm). Make sure you have a pan large enough to create a steamer with 1 inch (2.5 cm) of water inside. Give the batter a good stir to incorporate any flour settled at the bottom of the bowl. Unless they are non-stick, coat the inside of each tin or bowl with vegetable oil. Fill each with 1 heaping tablespoon of batter. Cover the steamer, allowing a small gap for some steam to escape. As moisture accumulates, wipe any that forms inside of the lid. Steam until the batter is set, 5 to 8 minutes. Carefully remove the muffin pan or bowls from the steamer. Remove the rice cakes from the pan or bowls and transfer to a serving platter. To serve, spoon the mung bean paste, dried shrimp, and pork belly over the rice cakes and drizzle with Green Onion Oil.

Rice Pyramid Dumplings

Bánh Giò

Makes 8 Dumplings
Prep time: 1 hour
Cook time: 1 hour

For the dough:
2 cups (280 g) cornstarch
1 cup (140 g) rice flour
1 tablespoon potato starch
4 cups (1 liter) high quality chicken broth
3 cups (750 ml) water
2 cups (500 ml) high quality pork stock
1 tablespoon vegetable oil

For the filling:
1 tablespoon vegetable oil
½ cup (70 g) chopped shallots
1 yellow onion, diced
1 lb (500 kg) ground pork
1 tablespoon freshly ground black pepper
2 teaspoons sugar
½ teaspoon fish sauce
1 teaspoon oyster sauce
1½ oz (40 g) dried wood ear mushrooms, soaked in warm water for 15–20 minutes, drained, and finely chopped
2 cloves garlic, minced
2 teaspoons cornstarch dissolved in 2 teaspoons water (slurry)

These dumplings are always a treat, particularly because I know firsthand how difficult it can be to master them. When I first started cooking—long before I went to culinary school—I'd never make a recipe with more than half a dozen ingredients. I now understand and appreciate the intrigue of complex recipes—especially those like these rice pyramids, which, in themselves hold and preserve Vietnam's identity.

1 For the dough: Sift the cornstarch, rice flour and potato starch into a large bowl. Whisk in the broth, water, stock and vegetable oil to form a smooth batter. Set aside for 1 hour.

2 Strain the batter through a mesh strainer into a large saucepan. Set over high heat, stirring constantly, until it becomes thick, 8–10 minutes. (Lower the temperature slightly if lumps begin to form.) Once the dough is about the consistency of cake frosting, remove the saucepan from the heat. Continue stirring for 30 more seconds; set aside to cool.

3 For the filling: Preheat the oil in a large skillet over medium-high heat. Add the shallot and onion and cook until lightly brown. Add the ground pork, pepper, sugar, fish sauce and oyster sauce. Sauté until the pork is almost cooked through. Add the mushroom and garlic and cook for another 1–2 minutes. Raise the heat to high. Add the slurry to the pork mixture. Once the liquid starts to bubble, reduce the heat to medium-low. Simmer, stirring, until the sauce is thickened and the pork is cooked through.

4 To assemble: Bring a large pot of water to a boil. Add the banana leaves and boil until pliable, about 2–3 minutes. Remove from the water, let cool, and pat dry.

5 Lay out the banana leaves (shiny side up), each over its own larger piece of foil. If space allows, it's best to lay out all the leaves at once so you can evenly distribute the dough and the filling on each banana leaf. Place approximately 1 tablespoon of the dough in the center

To assemble:
- 10–12 banana leaves, each 9 × 9 in (23 × 23 cm), blanched until pliable
- 10–12 pieces of aluminum foil, each 11 × 11 in (28 × 28 cm)
- 8 quail eggs, soft boiled and peeled

of each banana leaf. Flatten the dough into roughly the shape of a 3-inch (8-cm) circle. Gently press an indentation in the center of each circle to hold the filling. This will be the base of the pyramid. Put 2 tablespoons of filling in the very center of each piece of dough. Top the filling with one quail egg. Use the banana leaves to form pyramid shapes with square bases. Pull the leaves in tightly to ensure good coverage of the dough, while continuing to form the pyramid shapes. Wrap each dumpling securely with foil.

6 Steam the dumplings over boiling water for 40 to 45 minutes, or until an inserted skewer comes out mostly clean (some dough sticking to the skewer is okay). Let the dumplings cool enough to remove the foil and banana leaves. Serve warm.

Rice Paper Pizza
Bánh Tráng Nướng

Makes 4 Servings
Prep time: 15 mins
Cook time: 10–15 mins

4 eggs
4 green onions (scallions), sliced
8 oz (250 g) ground pork
2 cloves garlic, minced
2 teaspoons dried shrimp powder
1 teaspoon chili paste
½ teaspoon sugar
¼ teaspoon freshly ground black pepper
8 rice paper sheets
¼ cup (60 g) mayonnaise
¼ cup (60 g) sweet chili sauce
¼ cup (5 g) coarsely chopped coriander leaves (cilantro)
¼ cup (15 g) fried shallot

These crispy rice paper pizzas are a huge crowd pleaser, and they're so easy to make. As with most dishes in Vietnam, the ingredients vary region to region, but if there was ever a recipe that was safe for improvisation, this is it. Feel free to swap in your own favorite ingredients for the toppings.

1 In a small bowl, whisk together the eggs and green onions. Set aside.

2 Set a skillet over medium heat. Add the ground pork, garlic, shrimp powder, chili paste, sugar and pepper to the skillet and cook until the pork is browned and cooked through, about 5–10 minutes. Set aside.

3 If grilling, preheat the grill to medium-low and oil the grill to avoid sticking. If cooking in a pan, set a non-stick pan (without oil) over medium-low heat.

4 Wet one sheet of rice paper and adhere it to a dry one. Place the stacked sheets, dry side down, onto the grill or pan, and press down gently to keep the papers from bubbling or curving up. Cook, rotating occasionally to cook evenly, until opaque. Pour approximately ¼ of the egg mixture into the center of the rice papers, gently spreading the eggs to the edges. Quickly spoon the pork mixture over the eggs. Cook uncovered until the eggs are done, the topping is heated, and the rice paper is crispy. Repeat the process with the remaining 3 pizzas.

5 Combine the mayonnaise and sweet chili sauce in a bowl, and then add the mixture to a squeeze bottle. Drizzle each pizza with the mayonnaise and sweet chili sauce mixture. Top with coriander leaves and fried shallot, and serve warm. To enjoy, fold the pizza in half or slice.

Sticky Rice with Toppings
Xôi Mặn Thập Cẩm

Makes 4 Servings
Prep time: 8–10 hours
    (includes soaking)
Cook time: 45–50 mins

1½ cups (300 g) sticky rice
2 teaspoons turmeric,
    divided
¾ teaspoon salt, divided,
    plus more to taste
2 teaspoons full fat
    coconut milk
2 teaspoons high quality
    chicken stock
2 teaspoons sugar
½ cup (100 g) dried split
    mung beans, rinsed and
    soaked overnight
4 teaspoons chicken fat,
    warmed
Fried shallot, for garnish
Additional toppings, such
    as quail eggs, bean
    sprouts, etc. (optional)

Xôi means "rice," while *xèo* is an impolite way of telling someone to go away. Sticky rice is pure comfort food, appropriate for any time of the day—think of it as the shrimp and grits of Vietnam. Word to the wise: don't omit the chicken fat, because that's what makes this dish special.

1 Place the rice in a bowl, add 1 teaspoon of the turmeric, cover with cold water, stir to combine, and soak overnight.

2 Drain the rice, season with ½ of the teaspoon salt, stir to combine, and place in a steamer basket. In a large pot, add a couple inches of water, insert the steamer basket, cover and steam until soft, stirring halfway through cooking, about 25–30 minutes total. Add the coconut milk, chicken stock, sugar and the remaining turmeric. Mix well and steam for 2–3 more minutes. Remove from the heat and stir again.

3 Steam the soaked mung beans until soft, about 15 minutes. Add the mung beans and the remaining ¼ teaspoon of the salt to a food processor and process until smooth. When cool enough to handle, form into two balls and thinly slice.

4 To serve, spoon the sticky rice onto a plate or into a bowl. Top the rice with the mung-bean-ball slices and other optional toppings of your choosing. Drizzle with chicken fat and garnish with fried shallot.

Pho Rolls
Phở Cuốn

Makes 10–14 Rolls
Prep time: 2½–3 hours
   (includes marinating)
Cook time: 30–35 mins

For the rice-noodle
   sheet batter:
1 cup (140 g) rice flour
1 cup (120 g) tapioca flour
½ teaspoon salt
2 cups (500 ml) water
Vegetable oil, as needed

For the beef filling:
1 lb (500 g) beef sirloin,
   thinly sliced against
   the grain
2 bunches green onions
   (scallions), chopped
1 carrot, shredded
1 teaspoon oyster sauce
1 teaspoon sesame oil
1 teaspoon peeled and
   minced fresh ginger
1 teaspoon dark soy sauce
½ teaspoon five spice
   powder
¼ teaspoon salt
½ teaspoon freshly ground
   black pepper
1 teaspoon sugar

To assemble and serve:
Mixed greens
Perilla leaves
Coriander leaves (cilantro)
Soy sauce

These rolls are a unique spin on phở, the staple Vietnamese noodle soup. Just like the soup, this indispensable dish was born in Hanoi.

1 For the rice-noodle sheets: Sift the rice flour, tapioca flour and salt into a large mixing bowl and whisk to combine. Add the water and whisk until there are no lumps. Let the batter rest for 1–2 hours.

2 Warm a plate in the steamer for 2 minutes or until hot. Lightly oil the plate. Stir the batter. Ladle over just enough batter to cover the base of the plate. Roll the plate around to spread out the batter, if needed. Steam until firm, about 4–5 minutes. Peel off the rice-noodle sheet by running a spatula around its perimeter. Repeat with the remaining batter; set the rice sheets aside.

3 For the beef filling: Place the sirloin in a large bowl. Add the green onion, carrot, oyster sauce, sesame oil, ginger, soy sauce, five spice powder, salt, pepper and sugar, and toss to coat thoroughly. Set aside to marinate for 30 minutes.

4 Set a medium skillet over medium-high heat. Add the beef mixture and cook just until no longer pink.

5 To assemble and serve: Place one rice sheet on a flat surface. Evenly top with mixed greens, perilla leaves, coriander leaves and beef filling. Lift up one end and roll it up, gently but tightly. Repeat with the remaining rice sheets and filling. Serve immediately, or cool. Provide soy sauce alongside for dipping.

Thick Meat Cake Sandwiches

Bánh Giầy Giò

Makes 10 Servings
Prep time: 1½ hours
(plus chilling overnight)
Cook time: 1 hour, 20 mins

For the meat cake:
2 lbs (1 kg) ground pork (80/20), ground twice, if possible
3 teaspoons fish sauce
1 teaspoon vegetable oil
½ teaspoon salt
1 teaspoon ground white pepper
2 teaspoons sugar
1 clove garlic, minced
4 teaspoons ice water
1 teaspoon potato starch
¾ teaspoon baking powder

For the dough and assembly:
10 banana leaves, approximately 14 × 14 in (36 × 36 cm), cleaned
2 tablespoons vegetable oil, plus more as needed
1 lb (500 g) glutinous rice flour
2 teaspoons rice flour
½ teaspoon salt
1¾ cups (425 ml) cold water

Back in the days when the prevailing wisdom was that the Earth was square, these round cakes symbolized Heaven. This dish is traditionally used to express gratitude to the dead—a reminder of the critical importance of the enduring connections between food and culture in Vietnam.

1 For the meat cake: Place the pork, along with one large and one small mixing bowl, in the freezer for one hour prior to using. (Keep them cold at all times while preparing this recipe.)

2 Remove the pork and the chilled bowls from the freezer. In the large chilled bowl, combine the pork, fish sauce, oil, salt, pepper, sugar and garlic, and mix thoroughly. In the small chilled bowl, mix the water, potato starch and baking powder. Fold the potato starch mixture into the pork mixture until thoroughly incorporated. Cover the bowl and refrigerate overnight.

3 When ready to prepare, bring a steamer to a boil. While keeping the pork cold, work in small batches and place the pork mixture in a food processor and pulse until it looks smooth and glossy. Divide the pork into two plastic bags and place in the freezer until firm and manageable, but not frozen. Remove the bags from the freezer one at a time to shape the cakes into logs that are slightly smaller than the width of the banana leaves. Lay out 6 of the banana leaves, shiny-side up, next to each other on a work surface so there are three leaves for each log. Roll the banana leaves to wrap each pork log, covering all sides. Cut off any excess banana leaf, tie the rolls loosely with twine to secure their shapes, and then wrap them securely with plastic wrap. Steam until the internal temperature reaches 165°F (75°C). Remove and allow to cool.

4 For the dough and assembly: Cut the remaining 4 banana leaves into 3-inch (8-cm) circles. Brush each circle lightly with oil and lay on a steamer tray about 1 inch (2.5 cm) apart from each other. Set aside.

5 Sift the glutinous rice flour, rice flour and salt into a large mixing bowl. Slowly incorporate the water and 2 tablespoons of oil. With a spoon or spatula, combine well until the mixture can be formed into a soft ball. Pinch off a piece of dough and roll it into the shape of a golf ball. Place the ball onto a banana leaf circle, gently press the dough ball to flatten it slightly, but not too much, about ½-inch (1-cm) as it will flatten further when cooked. Repeat with the remaining dough and banana leave circles. Arrange the flattened dough balls on a tray and place the tray in a preheated steamer. Steam until the dough is completely opaque, 7–10 minutes (over-steaming will cause it to flatten too much). Remove the tray from the steamer and set aside.

6 Slice the meat cake into 10 slices. Place a slice of meat cake between two pieces of dough. Serve immediately or at room temperature.

Coconut Rice Cake with Toasted Shrimp Flakes

Bánh Đúc Tôm Cháy

Makes 6 Servings
Prep time: 20 mins
Cook time: 50 mins

For the rice cake batter:
Vegetable oil, as needed
2 cups (280 g) rice flour
¼ cup (30 g) tapioca flour
½ teaspoon salt
1 teaspoon sugar
2 cups (500 ml) water
¾ cup (185 ml) full fat
    coconut milk

To serve:
Green Onion Oil (see
    page 31)
Fried onions
Shrimp flakes
Dipping Sauce (see
    page 31)

In Vietnam, rice is a staple, and if you substitute a different element for a rice ingredient (for instance wheat flour or almond flour rather than rice flour) you will instantly lose all connection to the history of the dish. These rice cakes freeze well, so consider making a big batch.

1 For the rice cake batter: Brush an 8 × 8-inch (20 × 20-cm) baking dish with oil. Sift the rice flour, tapioca flour, salt and sugar together into bowl. Add the water and coconut milk to the dry ingredients and whisk until there are no lumps. Strain the batter into a medium saucepan. While whisking, heat the mixture over medium-low heat until the batter starts to thicken and all of the liquid is absorbed. Transfer the batter to the oiled baking dish. Tap the dish lightly on the counter to remove any air bubbles. Cover and place in the steamer on high for 20 minutes. Remove the cake from steamer. Let cool for at least 30 minutes.

2 To serve: Run a knife around the edge of the cake to loosen it from the dish. Invert the cake onto a cutting board. Cut with an oiled wavy knife into the desired shapes and sizes. Serve drizzled with Green Onion Oil and scattered with fried onions and shrimp flakes, with Dipping Sauce on the side.

Mango Salad
Nộm Xoài Xanh

Makes 4 Servings
Prep time: 15 mins

3 tablespoons sugar
3 tablespoons fish sauce
3 tablespoons fresh lime juice
3 tablespoons water
1 tablespoon sesame oil
1½ cups (245 g) diced mango
1½ cups (190 g) diced and seeded cucumber
2 tablespoons minced shallots
2 tablespoons coarsely chopped fresh coriander leaves (cilantro)
2 tablespoons crushed peanuts

The very first mango in Vietnam was referred to as *tây*, meaning "foreigner" or "West"—appropriate, because the French introduced the mango to the area in the 1940s. Today, the most popular Hanoi neighborhood for non-nationals is Hồ Tây ("West Lake").

Mangoes that grow in Vietnam, *quả xoài*, are unlike most other varieties. Uniquely delicious, sweet as candy, they're available year-round. I seek out dishes that feature them. I love the harmonious combination of the flavors in the following recipe: ingredients merge to create a simple, light meal that's great on its own or served with a bowl of rice, noodles or mixed greens.

1 In a small bowl, whisk together the sugar, fish sauce, lime juice, water and sesame oil to make the dressing.

2 In a large bowl, combine the mango, cucumber, shallot and coriander leaves. Pour the dressing over the salad and stir to coat.

3 Top with the crushed peanuts and serve.

Vietnamese Carrot & Cabbage Salad
Nộm Bắp Cải

Makes 4 Servings
Prep time: 15 mins

3 tablespoons sweet chili sauce

2 tablespoons fresh lime juice

2 tablespoons fish sauce

1 tablespoon honey

½ tablespoon peeled and grated fresh ginger

¼ white cabbage, shredded

3 large carrots, cut into thin matchsticks

½ bunch fresh Vietnamese mint, coarsely chopped

½ bunch fresh coriander leaves (cilantro), coarsely chopped

½ cup (70 g) crushed peanuts

The more I travel in Vietnam, the more I realize how differently the same recipes are prepared depending on the region where they're cooked. This salad was served as an appetizer at one of the first restaurant meals I enjoyed in Hanoi, and to this day, I distinctly remember tasting each ingredient in every bite.

1 In a medium bowl, mix the sweet chili sauce, lime juice, fish sauce, honey and ginger to make the dressing. Add the cabbage, carrot, mint and coriander leaves to the bowl and toss to coat.

2 Top with the crushed peanuts and serve.

Green Papaya Salad with Dried Shrimp & Peanuts
Nộm Đu Đủ

Makes 4 Servings
Prep time: 15–20 mins

1 cup (50 g) dried shrimp (any size), soaked in hot water for 10 minutes (optionally substitute fresh shrimp, peeled, deveined and cooked)

¼ cup (65 ml) fresh lime juice

¼ cup (65 ml) fish sauce

3 tablespoons honey

1 tablespoon toasted sesame oil

1 tablespoon minced garlic

⅛ teaspoon sweet chili sauce

¼ teaspoon salt

½ green papaya, shredded

2 cups (300 g) halved grape tomatoes

¼ cup (40 g) shredded carrots

¼ cup (20 g) shredded white cabbage

¼ cup (10 g) coarsely chopped fresh Vietnamese mint

¼ cup (10 g) coarsely chopped fresh coriander leaves (cilantro)

½ cup (70 g) crushed peanuts

Many recipes in Vietnamese cuisine are complex and time consuming—both in their preparation and cooking. This is an exception, and in my opinion, quick, tasty recipes like this add a nice balance.

1 Drain the soaked shrimp and pat dry with paper towels to remove excess moisture.

2 In a large bowl, mix the lime juice, fish sauce, honey, sesame oil, garlic, sweet chili sauce and salt to make the dressing. Add the shrimp, papaya, tomatoes, carrot, cabbage, mint and coriander leaves to the bowl and toss to coat.

3 Top with the crushed peanuts and serve.

Makes 6 Servings
Prep time: 20 mins
Cook time: 1 hour, 45 mins–2 hours,
    15 mins

For the pig's ears:
1 lb (500 g) pig's ears,
    hair removed, sliced ½-in
    (1-cm) thick
One 4-in (10-cm) piece fresh ginger,
    peeled and sliced
2 green onions (scallions), cut into
    2-in (5-cm) segments
2 shallots, halved
4 star anise
2 cinnamon sticks
¼ cup (65 ml) rice wine vinegar
¼ cup (65 ml) soy sauce
Water, as needed

For the salad:
4 oz (100 g) dried rice noodles
    (vermicelli)
2–4 bird's eye chili peppers
One 2-in (5-cm) segment of
    lemongrass, white part only,
    finely chopped
4 cloves garlic
2 teaspoons annatto oil
1 teaspoon sesame oil
1 tablespoon chicken stock
2 limes, juiced
1 teaspoon soy sauce
1 teaspoon black vinegar
½ teaspoon salt
1 teaspoon sugar
2 carrots, shredded
1 cup (20 g) coriander leaves
    (cilantro)
1 cup (20 g) Thai basil leaves
1 cup (20 g) perilla leaves
¼ cup (35 g) cashews, chopped

Pig's Ear Salad
Gỏi Tai Heo

Some ingredients, like mushrooms and salmon, tend to be rather forgiving when you cook. Pig's ears are on the opposite end of the spectrum, so cooking this delicacy takes practice to perfect.

1 For the pig's ears: In a large pot, combine the pig's ears, ginger, green onion, shallots, star anise, cinnamon, vinegar and soy sauce. Add enough water to cover the ingredients by about 2 inches (5 cm). Set over high heat, bring to a boil, and boil for 15 minutes. Cover the pot, reduce the heat to low, and braise whole for 1–2 hours, until the ears are tender. Drain, discarding the liquid. Cut the pig ears along the gristle into small strips. Set aside.

2 For the salad: Prepare the rice noodles according to the package instructions. Drain, rinse with cold water, and set aside.

3 Grind the chili peppers, lemongrass and garlic into a rough paste with a mortar and pestle. In a large mixing bowl, whisk together the paste, annatto and sesame oils, stock, lime juice, soy sauce, vinegar, salt and sugar. Whisk until the sugar is dissolved.

4 Add the noodles, carrot, pig's ears and herbs to the dressing. Toss to coat well. Serve at room temperature, topped with the chopped cashews.

Vietnamese Sizzling Pancakes

Bánh Xèo

Makes 6 Pancakes
Prep time: 1 hour, 15 mins
Cook time: 20–25 mins

For the pancake batter:
1 cup (140 g) rice flour
⅓ cup (45 g) all-purpose flour
1½ teaspoons turmeric
½ teaspoon salt
1½ cups (375 ml) water
½ cup (125 ml) full fat coconut milk
3 green onions (scallions), thinly sliced

To complete:
Annatto oil, as needed
½ yellow onion, thinly sliced
¾ lb (350 g) pork belly, sliced
½ lb (250 g) small shrimp (51/60), peeled
6 green onions (scallions), sliced
½ cup (100 g) dried split mung beans (soaked overnight)
2 cups (200 g) fresh bean sprouts, ends trimmed
1 cup (210 g) mixed greens
½ bunch perilla leaves
½ bunch mint, stems removed
½ bunch coriander leaves (cilantro), stems removed
Dipping Sauce (see page 31)

The word *xèo* in this recipe's title is a nod to the sizzling sound the batter makes as it hits the hot pan. You'll find these crispy Vietnamese crêpes all over Vietnam. It's a quintessential street-food dish that's flavorful and fun to eat. There are good and bad dishes at restaurants everywhere in the world. If you don't enjoy this dish the first time you have it, keep trying it at other places until you find someone who does it well, as you are sure to enjoy it!

1 For the pancake batter: Sift the rice flour, flour, turmeric and salt together into a large mixing bowl. Add the water and coconut milk, and whisk until no lumps remain. Stir in the green onion and set aside for 1 hour.

2 To complete: Heat 2 tablespoons of annatto oil in a large skillet over medium-high heat until shimmering. Add the onion, pork and shrimp and cook for 2–3 minutes, stirring occasionally, until almost cooked through. Add the green onion and cook for another 1–2 minutes. Remove from pan and set aside.

3 Pour about ½ cup of batter into the pan, tilting the pan quickly to create an even layer. Add more batter if there isn't enough to coat the pan. Add mung beans and sprouts. Continue by adding ⅙ of the pork and shrimp mixture. Lower the heat to medium. Cover the skillet and cook until the batter has cooked slightly, and the edges have become translucent, 2–3 minutes. Remove the lid, lower the heat to medium-low, and continue cooking until the pancake becomes crispy, 5–7 minutes. Fold the pancake in half and transfer to a plate. Repeat with the remaining batter. Serve warm with mixed greens, herbs and Dipping Sauce on the side.

Stuffed Pancakes with Pork Sausage
Bánh Cuốn

Makes 4–6 Servings
Prep time: 1 hour, 15 mins
Cook time: 20–25 mins

For the pancake batter:
7 oz (200 g) rice flour
2 oz (50 g) tapioca flour
½ teaspoon salt
2½ cups (600 ml) cold
    water

For the pork mixture:
2 tablespoons vegetable
    oil, plus more as
    needed
4 cloves garlic, minced
4 shallots, diced
1 bunch green onions
    (scallions), sliced
10 oz (330 g) pork, minced
4 dried wood ear mush-
    rooms, soaked in cold
    water for 2 hours,
    drained, and thinly
    sliced
2 teaspoons fish sauce
1 teaspoon oyster sauce
1 teaspoon sugar
½ teaspoon salt
½ teaspoon white pepper
Fried onions
Dipping Sauce (see
    page 31)
Meat cakes, for serving
    (optional) (see page 50)

In Hanoi, these stuffed pancakes are so popular that you'll probably have to wait in line for them. Creative inspiration may come from anywhere, but when I'm inspired by a food like *bánh cuốn*, my response is warmer than usual.

1 For the pancake batter: sift the rice flour, tapioca flour and salt together into a bowl. Add the water and whisk together until there are no lumps. Set aside to rest for 1 hour.

2 For the pork mixture: Heat the oil in a nonstick pan set over medium heat until shimmering. Add the garlic, shallot and green onion, and sauté until fragrant. Add the pork, mushroom, fish sauce, oyster sauce, sugar, salt and pepper. Continue cooking until the pork is cooked through, about 5–10 minutes. Set aside.

3 To complete: Lightly brush a plate with oil. Coat a large nonstick pan with oil and set over medium heat. Add 2–3 tablespoons of batter to the pan, rolling the pan in a circular motion to spread the batter to cover the base of the pan. Cover the pan with a lid and cook for 30 seconds. Slide the cooked pancake onto the oiled plate. Add 1 tablespoon of the pork mixture to the lower third of each pancake, fold the 2 sides in to cover the filling, and roll the pancake away from you to form a roll. Repeat this process with the remaining batter and pork mixture, adding oil to the pan as necessary. To serve, top the stuffed pancakes with fried onions and serve with Dipping Sauce on the side. Serve alone or with meat cakes and noodles.

Tofu, Pork Belly & Rice Noodles with Shrimp Sauce

Bún Đậu Mắm Tôm

Makes 4 Servings
Prep time: 20 mins
Cook time: 15–20 mins

8 oz (250 g) dried rice noodles (vermicelli)
14 oz (425 g) soft tofu, cut into 1-in (2.5-cm) cubes
2 teaspoons corn flour
½ teaspoon salt
¼ teaspoon ground white pepper
Vegetable oil, for frying

For the shrimp sauce:
2 teaspoons fermented shrimp paste (*mam tom*)
2 teaspoons sugar
1½ tablespoons fresh lime or lemon juice
4 cloves garlic, minced
1–2 bird's eye chili peppers, thinly sliced

10 oz (330 g) pork belly, boiled, thinly sliced
1 cup (20 g) perilla leaves
1 cup (20 g) Thai basil leaves

Shrimp paste is an essential ingredient in many Asian dishes, and sometimes, it's okay to substitute for it or omit an ingredient—this is not one of those times. The two teaspoons of shrimp paste in this dish are key to its flavor profile.

1 Prepare the rice noodles according to the package instructions. Drain, rinse with cold water, and set aside.

2 Pat the tofu dry with paper towels to remove excess moisture. Combine the corn flour, salt and pepper. In large pan, preheat oil over medium-high heat until shimmering. Working in batches, toss the tofu lightly in the corn flour mixture to coat and then deep fry until golden in color and crispy on the outside.

3 For the shrimp sauce: In a small bowl, whisk together the shrimp paste, sugar and lime or lemon juice until the sugar is dissolved. Mix in the garlic and garnish with chili pepper.

4 Serve the noodles, fried tofu, pork belly, shrimp sauce and herbs, all separately in serving bowls, or plated with sauce on the side.

Beef Rolls in Betel Leaves

Bò Cuốn Lá Lốt

Makes 8 Servings
Prep time: 25 mins
Cook time: 15–20 mins

For the beef mixture:
1 lb (500 g) ground beef
2 teaspoons curry powder
1 teaspoon sugar
1 teaspoon freshly ground black pepper
1 teaspoon salt
1 teaspoon fish sauce
2 cloves garlic, minced
1 shallot, minced
1 lemongrass stalk, minced

1 lb (500 g) dried rice noodles (vermicelli)
Green Onion Oil (see page 31)
40 betel leaves
½ cup (70 g) roasted peanuts, chopped
Dipping Sauce (see page 31)

When I first moved to Vietnam, my chopstick skills weren't great—maybe you'd give me a six out of ten—so ordering foods like this allowed me to cheat a little because I could use my hands! It was for the best, in the end, because these stuffed leaves are parcels of deliciousness.

1 For the beef mixture: In a large bowl, combine the ground beef, curry powder, sugar, pepper, salt, fish sauce, garlic, shallot and lemongrass. Mix thoroughly and let marinate for 10 minutes.

2 Prepare the rice noodles according to the package instructions. Drain, rinse with cold water, and set aside.

3 Lay the betel leaves on a flat surface, shiny side down. Add 1–2 tablespoons of the beef mixture to the center of each leaf. Fold in the sides and roll into a cylinder shape. Repeat with the remaining ingredients. (Extra betel leaves can be cut into thin matchsticks and used as garnish.)

4 Preheat a grill to medium-high. Place the stuffed leaves on the grill; baste with the Green Onion Oil and rotate every 2 minutes to prevent the leaves from burning. Grill until the meat is cooked through, about 7–10 minutes total. Baste with the Green Onion Oil once more before serving. Serve warm, garnished with the chopped peanuts, with Dipping Sauce on the side.

Vegetarian options: Substitute ground chickpeas with rice for the ground beef. Substitute vegetarian oyster sauce for fish sauce in the beef mixture. Substitute half soy sauce and half crushed pineapple for the Dipping Sauce.

Crispy Pork & Shrimp Spring Rolls

Nem Rán

Makes 32 Rolls
Prep time: 30 mins
Cook time: 20–25 mins

For the noodle mixture:
3½ oz (85 g) dried rice noodles (vermicelli)
1 lb (500 g) ground pork
12 oz (350 g) small shrimp (51/60), cooked, peeled, and diced
3 large eggs, beaten
2 carrots, grated
6 oz (175 g) fresh bean sprouts, ends trimmed
5 wood ear mushrooms, diced
3 green onions (scallions), sliced
1 teaspoon sugar
2 teaspoons fish sauce
1 teaspoon salt
1½ teaspoons freshly ground black pepper

64 rice paper wrappers*
Vegetable oil, for frying

*Using one rice paper wrapper per roll instead of two is optional

Like most Vietnamese dishes, *nem rán* are typically made with locally available ingredients. So have fun, and use what's fresh and local to you for your filling. They can be made in large batches because they freeze well, so you can enjoy them as last-minute meals, anytime snacks or paired with Beef Rolls in Betel Leaves (page 69).

1 For the noodle mixture: Soak the rice noodles in cold water until soft (10–15 minutes). Drain and cut the noodles into 2-inch (5-cm) pieces. In a large bowl, combine the noodles, pork, shrimp, egg, carrot, bean sprouts, mushroom, green onion, sugar, fish sauce, salt and pepper.

2 In a shallow bowl filled with warm water, soak 2 rice paper wrappers at a time to soften until pliable. Remove from the water and place on a flat surface, keeping the wrappers stacked together. Place 1½–2 tablespoons of the noodle mixture into the center of the softened rice papers. Fold the bottom edge into the center, covering the filling. Fold in the left and right edges and roll the paper away from you to seal the roll. (The roll should be loose, but secure, because the filling will expand when frying.) Repeat with the remaining rice papers and filling.

3 Heat 2–3 inches (5– 8 cm) of oil in a large pot or skillet over medium heat. Line a large plate with paper towels. Fry the spring rolls in small batches until golden brown, turning as needed. Check to make sure center is cooked through. Transfer the fried rolls to the paper towel-lined plate. Serve warm.

Mini Savory Pancakes
Bánh Khọt

Makes 26–30 Pancakes
Prep time: 1 hour, 15 mins
Cook time: 20–25 mins

2⅓ cups (325 g) rice flour
¼ cup (35 g) cornstarch
¾ teaspoon salt
¾ teaspoon turmeric
3¼ cups (815 ml) water
1 cup (250 ml) coconut milk
¼ cup (50 g) dried split mung beans (soaked overnight)
1 lb (500 g) jumbo shrimp (26/30), peeled and deveined
Green Onion Oil (see page 31)
Dipping Sauce (see page 31)

I've enjoyed these light and delicate mini pancakes with friends as we watched the sunset on the beach in Da Nang, with Lady Buddha in the background. Is it that memory that makes me love them even more?

1 Sift the rice flour, cornstarch, salt and turmeric into a large mixing bowl. Add the water and coconut milk and whisk together until no lumps remain. Set aside for 1 hour.

2 Drain the mung beans. Steam until soft, about 15 minutes. Add the steamed mung beans, to a food processor. Blend until smooth.

3 Heat a large non-stick skillet over medium-high heat. Give the batter a quick stir. Pour 1½ tablespoon portions of batter spaced around the skillet, leaving enough room to ensure the pancakes do not touch. Top each pancake with one shrimp and ½ teaspoon of mung bean paste. Cover the pan with a lid and cook until the pancake and shrimp are cooked through, about 5 minutes. Transfer to a serving plate. Repeat with the remaining ingredients. Drizzle the pancakes with Green Onion Oil while they are still warm. Serve immediately, with Dipping Sauce on the side.

Fertilized Duck Eggs
Hột Vịt Lộn

Makes 4 Eggs
Prep time: 5 mins
Cook time: 30–40 mins

2 teaspoons salt, divided,
    plus more as needed
4 fertilized duck eggs (the
    shells should be thick
    and have no cracks)
1 teaspoon fresh lime juice
1 bird's eye chili pepper,
    seeded and finely
    chopped

Fertilized eggs contain duck embryos that range from 14 to 17 days old. After 17 days, embryos typically begin to form beaks and feathers. If you find your duck egg to be a little on the crunchy side, you've probably chosen an older egg and are detecting either cartilage or a beak.

1 Bring a medium pot of water to a boil with 1 teaspoon salt. Gently add the eggs to the boiling water, lower the heat to medium, cover the pot, and boil for 30 to 40 minutes, depending how soft you want the eggs. Remove the eggs and transfer to an ice bath until cool enough to handle.

2 Combine the lime juice, the remaining teaspoon of salt and chili pepper in a small serving ramekin.

3 Serve the eggs while still warm, wide-side up. To enjoy, tap the shell gently with a spoon to create an opening, taking care not to lose any of the broth inside the shell. Sip out the juices before peeling away rest of shell. Use the salt mixture for dipping.

Pork & Mushroom Stuffed Tofu
Đậu Phụ Nhồi Thịt

Makes 2–4 Servings
Prep time: 40–45 mins
(includes soaking)
Cook time: 15–20 mins

For the sausage filling:
6 oz (175 g) mild pork
    sausage
2 dried shiitake
    mushrooms, soaked
    in hot water for 30
    minutes and minced
¼ teaspoon sugar
¼ teaspoon sesame oil
¼ teaspoon peeled and
    minced fresh ginger

1¼ lbs (600 g) extra-firm
    tofu, cut into 1½–2-in
    (4–5-cm) cubes
3 tablespoons vegetable oil
Smoked soy sauce, for
    garnish

I've had this dish throughout Vietnam, as a street food snack, in a restaurant topped with tomato sauce, even in a stir-fry. I love it not only because of how simple and delicious it is, but because it's so flexible with how it's served. Meat substitutes also make this an easy dish to serve as vegan.

1 In a medium mixing bowl, mix all the sausage filling ingredients until well combined.

2 Gently pat dry the tofu cubes. Using a small spoon or melon baller, scoop out about 1 teaspoon from the center of each tofu cube (enough to make room to add the sausage filling), being careful not to cut all the way through.

3 Stuff each piece with sausage filling, creating a small mound and pressing lightly to ensure that the sausage doesn't fall out.

4 With the heat off, place the oil in a large non-stick skillet. Place the tofu in the pan, sausage side up, before turning on the heat. Bring the temperature up to medium and cook 5 to 6 minutes until the bottom is golden brown.

5 Flip each piece of tofu with a spatula, or chopsticks, and cook for another 5 to 6 minutes. Cover and continue cooking for 2 more minutes, ensuring that the pork is cooked through.

6 Remove from the pan, plate sausage-side up and drizzle with smoked soy sauce. Serve with white rice.

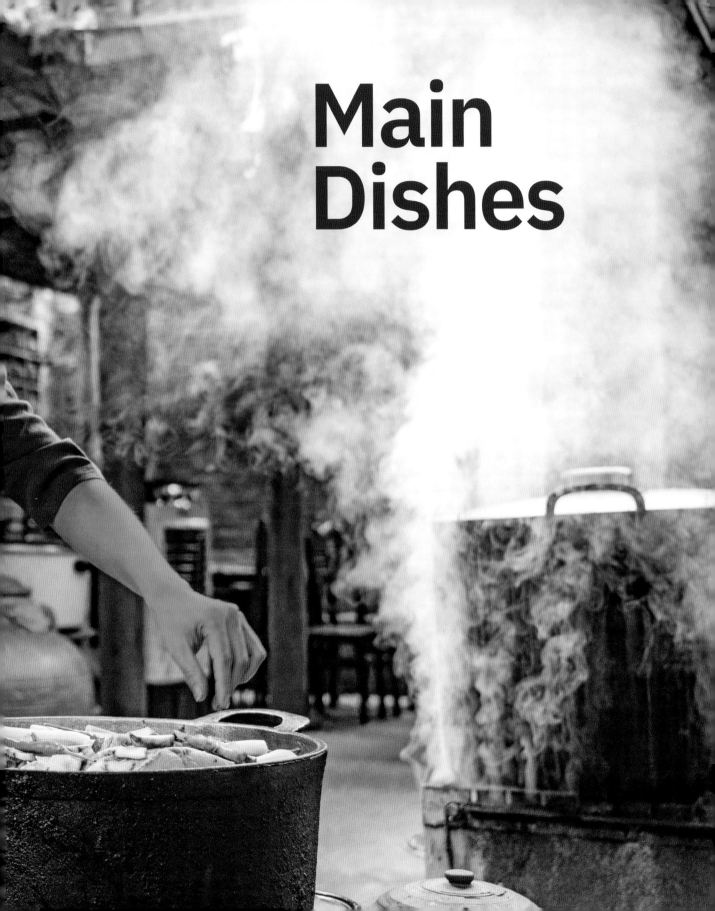

Main
Dishes

Eat to see the bowl, go to see the way.

—VIETNAMESE PROVERB

Main Dishes

Travel makes dining out an experience

In restaurants, you'll find motorcycle helmet racks instead of coat racks. Fresh lime juice and a little water are used for washing dishes, instead of hot water and soap. Scissors, not knives, are used to cut food. Waiters hand different menus with higher prices to people who aren't local. Many restaurants use pieces of old copy paper for napkins. In most dining establishments, if there isn't a trash can under your table, it's okay to throw your trash on the floor. Tipping is appreciated but not expected. Paying your bill by bank transfer is the norm for locals.

Travel goes well with a cold one

If suds are your thing, you can enjoy a glass of fresh beer—and I do mean fresh—while out exploring the streets of Vietnam. *Bia hơi* is served with street food and in small bars, and is meant to be consumed the same day it's produced—just as bread should be eaten. At around 3% ABV, it's light enough for you to enjoy a second glass with your meal and still find your way home without incident. The cost of beer? About 25 US cents per glass.

Travel helps to forge an adventurous palate

Look for the best bánh mì in Nam Dinh City—it's all about the bread! Canned tuna and squid are typical pizza toppings. Pork knees and duck blood are popular additions to soup; those ingredients are considered beneficial to one's health! You'll often be offered ice on the side when you order a custardy dessert. Drinks contain beans—black, white or kidney.

Travel provides an education in school culture

Schools use drums made of buffalo skin to signal the end of a class period rather than using alarms or bells. Students wear uniforms. But another reason why there's little variety in appearance among student bodies is that hairstyles are regulated. Class sizes can include up to 50 individuals! Teachers are honored both on Teacher's Day and the third day of Tet. Most schools don't have cafeterias or libraries; books for young people are relatively rare. Students generally have no idea who Oprah is but, they still talk about Obama.

Travel provides rest for the weary

People of every age, including me, take naps in the afternoon. At that moment, the country feels like one big kindergarten class during "quiet time." Locals participating in the *giấc ngủ trưa* (midday nap) are seemingly able to get comfortable wherever they are at the moment—including on top of their motorbikes! These breaks in the action are particularly important for workers performing manual labor.

◀ Assembling a pork meat bánh mì, accompanied by pâté and fried spring rolls

Baby Clam Rice Salad
Cơm Hến

Makes 4 Servings
Prep time: 20 mins
Cook time: 10–15 mins

For the anchovy sauce:
1 teaspoon vegetable oil
2 cloves garlic, minced
1 teaspoon minced lemongrass, white part only
2 teaspoons fresh lime juice
12 oz (350 ml) fermented anchovy sauce
2 teaspoons sugar
1¼ lbs (600 g) fresh pineapple, crushed
1 bird's eye chili pepper, chopped (optional)

For the baby clams:
12 oz (350 g) shelled baby clams, fresh or canned
1 teaspoon turmeric
1 teaspoon salt
1 teaspoon freshly ground black pepper
1 teaspoon sugar
1 tablespoon oyster sauce
2 teaspoons fish sauce
1 teaspoon annatto oil
2 cloves garlic, minced
1 teaspoon minced shallot
1 teaspoon minced lemongrass, white part only
1 bunch green onions (scallions), sliced
1 cup (20 g) chopped coriander leaves (cilantro)
¼ cup (35 g) roasted peanuts
¼ cup (15 g) fried shallot
Sesame rice crackers, for serving

Cơm Hến is named for the place where it was created, majestic Hen Island. This *cơm* (cooked rice) dish is made with basket clams—also known as Asian clams—from the island's beaches. There are lots of ingredients in this recipe, but they all play important roles in making a truly amazing dish!

1 For the anchovy sauce: In a small saucepan, heat the oil until shimmering. Sauté the garlic and lemongrass until fragrant. Add the lime juice, anchovy sauce and sugar. Whisk together until the sugar dissolves. Stir in the pineapple and bird's eye chili pepper, if using. Remove from the heat and set aside.

2 For the baby clams: In a small bowl, combine the clams, turmeric, salt, pepper, sugar, oyster sauce and fish sauce. In a large skillet, heat the annatto oil over medium heat until shimmering. Sauté the garlic, shallot, lemongrass and green onion until fragrant. Add the clam mixture to the skillet and continue cooking until heated through, 1–2 minutes. Remove from the heat and set aside to cool.

3 Add the coriander leaves, roasted peanuts and fried shallot to the clam mixture and stir to combine. Transfer to a serving bowl and serve at room temperature with sesame rice crackers and anchovy sauce on the side.

Soy Braised Fish
Cá Kho Tộ

Makes 4 Servings
Prep time: 10 mins
Cook time: 20–25 mins

2 lbs (1 kg) mild white fish
    steaks
Salt and freshly ground
    black pepper, as
    needed
1 tablespoon vegetable oil
2 shallots, minced
4 cloves garlic, minced
1 tablespoon fish sauce
2 teaspoons sugar
½ teaspoon dark soy sauce
1 cup (250 ml) coconut
    soda
2 cups (500 g) white rice,
    cooked
1 green onion (scallion),
    thinly sliced
2 bird's eye chili peppers,
    thinly sliced

I like to use catfish when making *cá kho tộ*, but any firm, mild, white fish will do. Often, when I travel within Vietnam, I'm invited to dine with my hosts, and this dish is what's served for dinner most often. A plate of it brings back warm and wonderful memories of many family dinners I've enjoyed throughout the country.

1 Lightly season the fish with salt and pepper. In a large skillet, heat the oil over medium-high heat until shimmering. Add the shallot and garlic and sauté until fragrant.

2 Add the fish steaks, fish sauce, sugar, soy sauce and soda to the skillet, and flip the fish steaks to coat them evenly in the braising liquid. Bring to a simmer and cook for 10 minutes. Flip the fish, cover the pan, and simmer until the fish is cooked through, about another 10 minutes. Serve warm with white rice, topped with any remaining liquid from the skillet. Garnish with green onion, chili pepper and black pepper, to taste.

Beef Noodle Soup
Phở Bò

Makes 4 Servings
Prep time: 15 mins
Cook time: 1 hour, 15 mins

For the broth:

2 yellow onions, peeled and halved lengthwise

3-in (7.5-cm) piece fresh ginger, peeled and halved lengthwise

4 star anise

5 whole cloves

4 cardamom pods

3 cinnamon sticks

2 teaspoons coriander seeds

2 teaspoons fennel seeds

2 quarts (1.9 liters) high quality pork stock

1 teaspoon brown sugar

1 teaspoon fish sauce

Salt, to taste

To serve:

7 oz (200 g) dried rice noodles (vermicelli)

½ lb (250 g) brisket (or flank steak or chuck roast), raw, thinly sliced against the grain

¼ cup (5 g) coriander leaves (cilantro), coarsely chopped

¼ cup (5 g) Vietnamese basil leaves, coarsely chopped

2 green onions (scallions), green parts only, sliced

2 limes, cut into wedges

1 bird's eye chili pepper, thinly sliced

Chili garlic sauce (optional)

Phở is to Vietnam what barbecue is to the United States: it's different depending on where you are in the country, and it's constantly evolving. Most historians believe phở was first developed in Hanoi and that it is a derivative of the French soup *pot au feu* (because the Vietnamese pronounce *feu* the same way they pronounce phở). Thus, the iconic dish phở is a local adaptation of a classic French soup. Wherever you go in Vietnam, you'll encounter a different version of this humble dish. In my opinion, what elevates a bowl of phở is a subtle overtone of cinnamon.

1 For the broth: Heat a dry cast iron pan over medium-high heat. Once hot, add the onion and ginger, cut-sides down, and sear until charred. Remove from the pan and set aside.

2 Heat a large pot over medium-high heat. Add the star anise, cloves, cardamom pods, cinnamon, coriander and fennel seeds. Toast, stirring frequently, until fragrant, about 3 minutes. Add the charred onion and ginger and pork stock to pot. Once the stock comes up to a simmer, cover the pot, reduce the heat to medium-low, and simmer for 30–40 minutes. Strain the mixture, return the stock to the pot, and bring it to a boil. Once the stock boils, remove it from the heat and stir in the brown sugar and fish sauce. Continue stirring until the sugar is dissolved. Add salt as needed.

3 Prepare the rice noodles according to the package instructions.

4 To serve: Divide the noodles between the serving bowls. Top each bowl with a portion of steak and herbs. Top with the hot broth, pouring it directly over the beef to cook it. Serve with the lime wedges, chili pepper, and chili garlic sauce (if using) on the side.

Banh Mi Sandwich
Bánh Mì

Makes 2 Servings
Prep time: 4 hours, 15 mins
(includes marinating)
Cook time: 10 mins

For the pork:
½ lb (250 g) pork shoulder or belly, thinly sliced
1 shallot, minced
1 lemongrass stalk, minced
1 tablespoon soy sauce
1 tablespoon fish sauce
1 tablespoon oyster sauce
1 tablespoon brown sugar
1 tablespoon minced garlic
½ teaspoon freshly ground black pepper
½ teaspoon five spice powder
½ teaspoon honey
½ teaspoon oil

For the pickled vegetables:
½ cup (125 ml) white vinegar
½ cup (125 ml) water
¼ cup (50 g) sugar
½ teaspoon salt
½ daikon radish, cut into thin matchsticks
1 small carrot, cut into thin matchsticks

For the sandwich:
2 small Vietnamese baguettes
2 tablespoons Vietnamese mayonnaise (or Kewpie brand)
1 tablespoon soy sauce
½ cucumber, cut lengthwise into thin strips
1 jalapeño pepper, sliced
Fresh coriander leaves (cilantro)

Throw everything you already know about bánh mì out the window, and just focus on the bread—it must be thin and crackly on the outside, and soft on the inside. The most popular variety of bánh mì is *bánh mì thịt*—the word *thịt* means "meat," but the variations are endless. Bánh mì with fried egg and pâté is often eaten for breakfast. A version with meatballs or barbecued pork could appear on your plate at lunch or dinner. One with ice cream and peanuts might be on a menu for dessert!

1 For the pork: In a large bowl, combine all of the pork section ingredients until mixed well and the pork is evenly coated. Cover and marinate in the refrigerator for 4 hours.

2 For the pickled vegetables (these can be prepared in advance): In a saucepan, combine the vinegar, water, sugar and salt. Bring to a boil, and then remove from the heat and let cool slightly. Place the radish and carrot in a jar or bowl. Completely cover with the vinegar mixture. Let sit for at least 1 hour.

3 Preheat the grill to medium-high heat. Using lightly greased aluminum foil or a grilling pan, grill the slices of pork for 3–5 minutes on each side until fully cooked.

4 Assemble the sandwiches: Slice the baguettes horizontally. Spread a thin layer of mayonnaise on the inside of the baguettes. Drizzle the soy sauce on top of the mayonnaise. Arrange the pork, cucumber and pickled vegetables evenly on the inside. Add jalapeños and coriander leaves, to taste.

Variations: *Bánh mì bì*: shredded pork with fish sauce; *Bánh mì bơ*: butter and sugar; *Bánh mì cá mòi*: sardines; *Bánh mì chà bông*: pork floss; *Bánh mì chả cá*: fish patty; *Bánh mì chả lụa*: pork sausage; *Bánh mì chay*: vegetarian, usually containing tofu (often served at Buddhist temples during special religious events).

Grilled Cheese with Durian Jam

Bánh Mì Nướng Phô Mai Với Mứt Sầu Riêng

Makes 4 Sandwiches
Prep time: 10 mins
Cook time: 40–45 mins

For the jam:
7–8 oz (200–250 g) durian meat
1 cup (250 ml) coconut milk
8 tablespoons sugar
½ teaspoon salt

For the sandwich:
4 tablespoons butter, unsalted, softened
8 slices of rustic bread, ⅜-in (1-cm) thick
8 slices white cheddar cheese
4 slices of Gruyere cheese
4 slices Havarti cheese

Ever since I tried Musang King, the king of durians, I have been on a quest to try to experiment with different durian dishes, everything from durian cappuccino to durian pizza. Musang King durians are candy-sweet, creamy, with hints of tropical fruits and vanilla. Durian is definitely an acquired tasted, but once you understand what it is everyone loves about it, you start to appreciate the different types of durians. So next time you are in Asia, seek out Musang King durians.

1 For the jam: In a medium bowl, place the durian meat, coconut milk, sugar and salt, and mix thoroughly.

2 In a medium non-stick pan over medium-low heat, add the durian mixture and stir constantly, 30–45 minutes, or until thickened to jam consistency. Set aside.

3 For the sandwich: Generously butter (using ½ tablespoon) one side of each slice of bread.

4 Heat a large skillet over low to medium-low heat and place two slices of bread, butter-side-down, in the skillet.

5 Place a slice of white cheddar, followed by a slice of Gruyere, and another slice of white cheddar, onto each bread slice in the skillet.

6 Top with a heaping tablespoon of the durian jam, spreading evenly.

7 Cover each stack with a piece of bread, buttered side up.

8 Cook until the bread is toasted and golden and cheese is melted, about 3 minutes per side. Prepare the remaining two sandwiches in the same way.

9 Slice each sandwich in half diagonally and serve while warm.

10 Store any unused jam in the refrigerator for up to a month.

Spicy Lemongrass Chicken
Gà Xào Sả Ớt

Makes 4 Servings
Prep time: 45 mins
(includes marinating)
Cook time: 10–12 mins

For the marinade:

1½ lbs (750 g) chicken breast and thigh meat, cut into 1-in (2.5-cm) cubes
4 teaspoons annatto oil, divided
2 teaspoons soy sauce
1 tablespoon brown sugar

2 teaspoons minced garlic
4 teaspoons minced shallots
10 lemongrass stalks, minced
1 teaspoon fish sauce
Salt, to taste
1 lemon
1 bird's eye chili pepper, thinly sliced
½ cup (30 g) fried shallot
2 green onions (scallions), thinly sliced
2 cups (500 g) cooked white rice

I first ordered this dish at a lunchtime spot tucked into a little alley in Hanoi. As I sat and enjoyed it in my little red plastic chair at a little red plastic table, I marveled that such a fragrant and flavorful dish was possible. You'll love the aromas the ingredients produce when you cook it.

1 In a shallow bowl, combine the chicken, 2 teaspoons of annatto oil, soy sauce, and brown sugar. Marinate in the refrigerator for 30 minutes.

2 In a medium skillet, heat the remaining annatto oil over medium-high heat until shimmering. Add the garlic, shallot, lemongrass and fish sauce and heat until fragrant. Remove the chicken from the marinade (discarding the excess marinade) and add it to the pan. Cook until the chicken is cooked through, about 7 minutes. Taste and add salt, if needed. Squeeze fresh lemon juice over the chicken. Garnish with the chili pepper, fried shallot and green onion, and serve warm with a side of white rice.

Mixed Instant Noodles
Bún Trộn Đậu Phụ

Bún trộn đậu phụ is so versatile, it welcomes substitutions: feel free to switch in your favorite vegetables or proteins. It's also great to make the parts of the recipe in advance and combine the noodles and dressing at the last minute before serving. Enjoy this dish hot or cold.

Makes 4 Servings
Prep time: 2 hours, 20 mins
(includes marinating)
Cook time: 15–20 mins

For the noodles:
2 teaspoons sesame oil
2 cloves garlic, minced
1 teaspoon peeled and grated fresh ginger
2 teaspoons soy sauce
2 teaspoons sugar
12 oz (350 g) firm tofu, cut into ½–1-in (1.25–2.5-cm) cubes
3 tablespoons vegetable oil
8 oz (250 g) dried vermicelli noodles or ramen
2 cups (180 g) green cabbage, shredded
1 carrot, shredded
2 green onions (scallions), thinly sliced
½ cup (10 g) coriander leaves (cilantro), chopped
1 cup (145 g) cooked shrimp (optional)
1 cup (145 g) cooked squid (optional)

For the dressing and garnish:
2 teaspoons sesame oil
2 teaspoons rice wine vinegar
1 teaspoon soy sauce
1 teaspoon sugar
Salt, to taste
½ cup (30 g) fried shallot
½ cup (70 g) roasted peanuts, chopped
1 lime, cut into wedges

1 In a mixing bowl, stir together the sesame oil, garlic, ginger, soy sauce and sugar. Add the tofu and marinate for 2 hours.

2 In a large skillet, heat 3 tablespoons vegetable oil over medium-high heat until shimmering. Remove the tofu from the marinade (reserving the marinade) and add the tofu to the pan. Sauté until golden brown, turning as needed. Add the reserved marinade and stir until well combined and heated through. Separate the cooked tofu from the marinade and set both aside to cool.

3 Cook the vermicelli noodles according to the package instructions; drain and rinse with cold water. In a large bowl, combine the cooked noodles, cabbage, carrot, green onion, coriander leaves and shrimp and/or squid (if using).

4 In a small mixing bowl, whisk together 1 teaspoon of the reserved tofu cooking oil, the sesame oil, rice wine vinegar, soy sauce and sugar, whisking until the sugar is dissolved. Taste and add salt, if desired.

5 Add the tofu and the dressing to the noodle salad and toss to coat thoroughly. Garnish each serving with the fried shallot, peanuts and lime wedges, and serve warm or at room temperature.

Quang Style Soup Noodles
Mì Quảng

Makes 8 Servings
Prep time: 20 mins
Cook time: 1 hour, 20 mins

For the broth:
1 lb (500 g) pork belly
½ lb (225 g) beef brisket
8 cups (1.75 liters) high quality, low sodium chicken stock
2 teaspoons annatto oil
1 onion, diced
2 shallots, thinly sliced
½ lb (225 g) medium large shrimp (36/40), peeled and deveined
1 bulb garlic, minced
½ lb (225 g) crabmeat
2 teaspoons salt
1 tablespoon sugar
2 teaspoons paprika
1 teaspoon white pepper
2 teaspoons fish sauce

When you try a new recipe, it may be tempting to substitute ingredients if you don't have the full list of ingredients on hand. I know—I've been there. For this dish, however, the Quảng noodles are really important, so look for them at a local Asian market or online.

Mì Quảng is known for its unusual noodles, which get their color from turmeric, and its complex and flavorful broth. Every time I make it, I'm transported back to the first time I tasted it, at the home of a friend in a tiny village outside of Hội An.

When you visit Vietnam, I urge you to try dishes in their locations of origin. To taste Quảng style noodles at the source, be sure you visit the Quảng Nam province in central Vietnam.

1 For the broth: Add the pork belly, beef brisket and chicken stock to a large stock pot and bring the stock to a boil. Cover, reduce to a simmer, and cook for 1 hour, skimming the fat as needed. Transfer the pork belly and brisket to a cutting board and allow them to cool slightly; remove the stock from the heat and leave it in the pot. Thinly slice the meat and set aside.

2 Heat the annatto oil in a deep skillet over medium heat until shimmering. Add the onion and shallot and sauté until fragrant, but not brown, 30–60 seconds. Add the sliced meat and sauté for 4 min. Add the shrimp and garlic; sauté for 2–3 more minutes. Add the crabmeat,

To serve:

1 lb (500 g) dried Quang noodles

2 cups (210 g) fresh bean sprouts, ends trimmed

1 banana flower, thinly sliced

4 green onions (scallions), thinly sliced

1 bunch Vietnamese mint

1 bunch coriander leaves (cilantro), coarsely chopped

4 large sesame rice crackers

2 limes, cut into wedges

8 bird's eye chili peppers, thinly sliced

salt, sugar, paprika and white pepper. Immediately remove the skillet from the heat, continuing to mix well. Set aside.

3 Bring the stock to a boil. Reduce to a simmer and add the contents of the skillet. Stir until combined. Simmer until the shrimp is fully cooked. Stir in the fish sauce. Adjust seasoning with additional sugar, salt and pepper, as needed.

4 To serve: Cook the noodles according to the package instructions. Drain, rinse in cold water, and set aside.

5 Add the Quang noodles to the bowls. Ladle the soup into the bowls, evenly distributing the meat, shrimp and crabmeat. Fill the bowl halfway with broth. Garnish with the sprouts, banana flower, green onion, mint, coriander leaves, rice crackers, lime wedges, and chili pepper.

Pork Cutlets with "Broken Rice"
Cơm Tấm

Makes 4 Servings
Prep time: 4–6 hours
(includes marinating)
Cook time: 25–30 mins

3 cloves garlic, minced
2 lemongrass stalks,
minced
1 shallot, minced
1½ teaspoons fish sauce
1 teaspoon oyster sauce
1 tablespoon vegetable oil
2 teaspoons soy sauce
1 teaspoon honey
1 teaspoon brown sugar
4 boneless pork cutlets
2 cups (400 g) broken rice
or short grain rice
2 cups (480 ml) water
Pinch of salt
2 teaspoons annatto oil
4 eggs, fried
Fried onions
Shredded pork skin
(optional)
Fish sauce

Optional sides:
Mixed vegetables
Cucumber slices
Steamed egg loaf

The combination of the pork's flavor and the softness of the broken rice makes this a crowd pleaser. It's one of the most popular recipes on my website—along with the most popular, phở (page 87) and spring rolls (page 37)—for good reason. You'll never get tired of it.

This dish is to south what phở is to the north. The word *cơm* means "cooked rice" and *tấm* means "broken." Traditionally, certain grains of rice were damaged—broken—during the milling process. These broken grains were sold cheaply, and this recipe became popular as a result.

1 In a shallow bowl, mix the garlic, lemongrass, shallot, fish sauce, oyster sauce, vegetable oil, soy sauce, honey and brown sugar until the sugar is dissolved. Add the pork and marinate for 4–6 hours in the refrigerator.

2 Rinse the rice and add it to a pot with the water and a pinch of salt. Bring to a boil, stir, cover, and reduce the heat to low. Cook for 15–20 minutes. Turn off the heat and let sit for 5 more minutes. Fluff with a fork.

3 Heat the annatto oil in a large skillet over medium-high heat until shimmering. Remove the pork from the marinade (discarding the marinade) and sear on one side until golden brown, about 4–5 minutes. Flip the pork and sear on the other aside. When the pork reaches an internal temperature of 135–140°F (57–60°C), remove it from the pan to rest and reach an internal temperature of 145°F (63°C). Serve the pork over the broken rice. Pair each serving with a fried egg. Pair with other sides, if using. Garnish with fried onions and shredded pork skin, if using. Serve with fish sauce on the side.

Vietnamese Chicken Curry
Cà Ri Gà

Makes 4 Servings
Prep time: 5 hours, 20 mins
(includes marinating)
Cook time: 40–45 mins

4–8 chicken drumsticks
2 teaspoons turmeric powder
2 teaspoons curry powder, divided
1 stalk lemongrass, cut into 1-in (2.5-cm) pieces, smashed
½ cup (125 ml) vegetable oil
1½ lbs (750 g) potatoes, peeled and cut into large chunks
2 cloves garlic, minced
1 large yellow onion, sliced
3 cups (750 ml) high quality chicken broth
3 cups (750 ml) high quality pork stock
2 teaspoons sugar
1 bay leaf
1 cup (250 ml) coconut milk
Salt, to taste
2 French baguettes, warmed

The terms Indochina or Indochine refer to the countries that sit between India and China—Vietnam, Laos, Cambodia, Thailand and Myanmar. Various inspirations from these unique cultures merged together to create their own amalgam. Using curry in Vietnamese dishes like *cà ri gà* is an excellent example of one influence. Just its name conjures up the visions, smells and tastes of a hot bowl of deliciousness.

1 Combine the drumsticks, turmeric powder, 1 teaspoon of the curry powder, lemongrass and vegetable oil in a shallow bowl. Cover and refrigerate for 5 hours. Separate the chicken and the lemongrass from the marinade and set aside.

2 Heat the oil in a large pot over high heat. Add the potatoes and fry until crispy and golden brown on the exterior (they will cook through later, in the broth). Set aside.

3 Heat the reserved marinade in a large skillet set over medium heat. Once the marinade is shimmering, add the lemongrass and garlic and sauté until fragrant. Add the chicken and onion and sear until the outside of the chicken is golden brown. Remove from the heat.

4 In another large pot, season the chicken and pork stock with the remaining curry, sugar, and bay leaf, and bring the mixture to a boil. Lower the temperature to medium and add the potatoes and the seared chicken and onion mixture. Simmer for 15–20 minutes, or until the chicken is cooked through. Add the coconut milk and bring the soup to a boil. Remove from the heat; taste and add salt, if needed. Serve warm with warmed French baguettes alongside.

Grilled Vietnamese Fish
Chả Cá Lã Vọng

Makes 4 Servings
Prep time: 40 mins
   (includes marinating)
Cook time: 10–15 mins

For the marinade:
1 tablespoon vegetable oil
2 teaspoons minced shallot
1 teaspoon minced garlic
1 teaspoon freshly ground
   galangal
1 teaspoon freshly ground
   turmeric
2 teaspoons fish sauce
1 teaspoon sugar
1 teaspoon salt
1 teaspoon shrimp paste
1½ lbs (750 g) halibut, cut
   into 1½-in (3.75-cm)
   pieces

To complete:
6 oz (175 g) dried rice
   noodles (vermicelli)
Rice flour, for dredging
3 tablespoons vegetable oil
Salt and freshly ground
   black pepper
14–16 green onions
   (scallions) cut into
   1–2-in (2.5–5-cm)
   pieces

This tasty, healthy dish, generally served family style, is a hallmark of Vietnamese cuisine. I fell in love with it at the restaurant where it was invented, Hanoi's Chả Cá Lã Vọng, and I still order it there often. But I also enjoy the version I make at home, using this recipe, just as much. The restaurant's name translates as *chả*, "grilled" or "fried"; *cá*, fish; and La Vong, is in honor of a former prime minister named Lu Wang (pronounced "La Vong").

Chả cá was often served to troops and neighbors during Vietnam's time under French rule. It's unlike most dishes in Vietnamese cuisine because it requires a two-part cooking process. The fish is first partially grilled, and then usually finished tableside using a portable hot plate. If you happen to own a hot plate, I recommend using it. It's a great way to involve everyone at the table in the preparation and it also helps keep the food warm. No matter what the approach, this is a delicious meal that can be served year-round in individual portions or family style.

2 cups (20 g) dill leaves and tender stems, coarsely chopped
¼ cup (5 g) perilla leaves
¼ cup (5 g) mint leaves
¼ cup (5 g) Thai basil leaves
Dipping Sauce (see page 31)
¼ cup (35 g) roasted unsalted peanuts

1 For the marinade: In a shallow bowl, mix together the oil, shallot, garlic, galangal, ground turmeric, fish sauce, sugar, salt and shrimp paste. Add the fish to the marinade, toss to coat well, cover, and marinate in the refrigerator for 30 minutes.

2 To complete: Prepare the rice noodles according to the package instructions. Drain, rinse with cold water, and set aside.

3 Add some rice flour to a shallow bowl. Transfer the fish from the marinade to a paper towel-lined plate and pat the fish pieces dry. In a large nonstick pan, preheat the oil over medium-high heat until shimmering. Working quickly, season the fish with salt and pepper, and then dredge the pieces in flour, shaking off any excess. Use tongs to gently add the fish to the pan. Cook until golden brown and cooked through, flipping once halfway through cooking, 4–5 minutes total. Add the green onions and dill and cook for about 30 more seconds. Remove from the heat, transfer to a serving bowl, and top with the perilla, mint and basil. Serve the fish warm with rice noodles, Dipping Sauce and peanuts.

Vegetarian options: Substitute firm tofu for the fish. Substitute fermented soybean paste for shrimp paste. Substitute 50/50 pineapple juice/soy sauce for the fish sauce.

Pork Belly & Eggs Simmered in Sweet Soy

Thịt Kho Tàu

Makes 4 Servings
Prep time: 10–15 mins
Cook time: 1 hour, 20 mins

1 teaspoon vegetable oil
1 shallot, thinly sliced
2 cloves garlic, thinly sliced
1 cup (250 ml) coconut water
1 cup (250 ml) high quality, low sodium pork stock
1 teaspoon brown sugar
½ teaspoon freshly ground black pepper
1½ lbs (750 g) pork belly, cut into 1½-in (3.75-cm) chunks
2 teaspoons fish sauce
1 tablespoon thick soy sauce
4 large eggs, soft boiled and peeled

This sweet and savory recipe is the ultimate Vietnamese comfort food dish. Whenever I make a big batch I always invite friends over to share—in addition to enjoying the food, they also get an opportunity to laugh at my attempts to speak Vietnamese.

1 Heat the oil in a medium pot over medium-high heat until shimmering. Add the shallot and garlic and cook until fragrant, 1–2 minutes (do not allow the garlic to burn). Add the coconut water and pork stock and bring the mixture to a boil. Add the brown sugar, pepper and pork, and bring back to boil. Cover the pot and lower the heat to a simmer for 1 hour. Skim fat from the surface of the stock as needed. Remove the pork from the liquid and set aside.

2 Bring the liquid to a boil and cook until reduced to ⅓ of its original volume. Add the fish sauce and thick soy sauce. Reduce the heat, return the pork to the sauce, and simmer for 10 minutes, uncovered. Add the eggs and simmer for 10 more minutes, making sure the eggs are covered in the liquid. To serve, slice the eggs into halves or quarters. Serve hot, with pork and juices from the pan.

Grilled Pork with Noodles
Bún Chả

Makes 4 Servings
Prep time: 20 mins
Cook time: 10–15 mins

For the sauce:
¼ cup (50 g) sugar
1 tablespoon fish sauce
¼ cup (65 ml) rice wine vinegar
¼ cup (65 ml) fresh
    lime juice
3 cloves garlic, minced
⅔ cup (160 ml) water

For the meatballs:
1½ lbs (750 g) ground pork
2 teaspoons fish sauce
2 teaspoons oyster sauce
1 tablespoon sugar
¼ cup (35 g) minced shallots
2 cloves garlic, minced
2 lemongrass stalks,
    white part only, minced
Pinch of salt and white pepper
1 tablespoon oil, for cooking

To serve:
8 oz (250 g) dried rice noodles
    (vermicelli)
1 cup (20 g) Vietnamese mint
    leaves
1 cup (20 g) Thai basil leaves
1 bird's eye chili pepper, thinly
    sliced
Lime wedges (optional)
Crispy Pork & Shrimp Spring Rolls
    (see page 71) (optional)

I've never met anyone who doesn't like *bún chả*. It's on my short list of what to make anytime I have company over.

1 For the sauce: In a small bowl, mix the sugar, fish sauce, vinegar, lime juice, garlic and water until the sugar is dissolved. Set aside.

2 For the meatballs: In a large mixing bowl, combine the pork, fish sauce, oyster sauce, sugar, shallot, garlic, lemongrass and the pinch of salt and white pepper. Mix until well combined. Use your hands to shape the mixture into 8 mini patties. Heat the oil in a skillet over medium-high heat until shimmering. Add the patties and cook until golden on the first side, about 2½ minutes. Flip and cook for 2 minutes on the other side.

3 To serve: Prepare the rice noodles according to the package instructions. Drain and rinse with cold water.

4 Serve the meatballs over the noodles, and spoon over a generous amount of sauce. Top with mint, basil and chili pepper, with lime wedges alongside, if using. Accompany with Crispy Pork & Shrimp Spring Rolls, if using.

Spicy Beef Stew
Bò Kho

Makes 6–8 Servings
Prep time: 2 hours, 20 mins
   (includes marinating)
Cook time: 1 hour, 45 mins

For the marinade:
2–2½ lbs (1–1.25 kg) brisket or
   boneless beef chuck, cut into 11
   2-in (5-cm) chunks
4 teaspoons fish sauce
5 cloves garlic, minced
3 teaspoons peeled and minced
   fresh ginger
2½ teaspoons five spice powder
1½ teaspoons brown sugar
1 teaspoon freshly ground
   black pepper
½ teaspoon liquid smoke

For the stew:
3 lemongrass stalks, cut into
   3-in (7.5-cm) lengths, smashed
1 cinnamon stick
2–4 star anise, whole
2 bay leaves
1 tablespoon annatto oil
2 yellow onions, thinly sliced
4 teaspoons tomato paste
6 cups (1.5 liters) high quality, low
   sodium vegetable stock
1 cup (250 ml) coconut water
1 teaspoon sweet paprika
5 large carrots, cut into
   1½-in (3.75-cm) chunks
1 teaspoon salt, plus more as needed
1 tablespoon dark soy sauce
⅓ cup (10 g) coarsely chopped
   coriander leaves (cilantro)
⅓ cup (10 g) coarsely chopped
   Thai basil leaves
2–3 baguettes, warmed

Hearty meals are uncommon in Vietnam, so when I find one I love, like this aromatic and flavorful stew, I become a devoted follower. I've never had a bowl of it without a warm baguette, and I never will.

1 For the marinade: In a large bowl, combine the beef, fish sauce, garlic, ginger, five spice powder, brown sugar, black pepper and liquid smoke. Toss to coat evenly and marinate in the refrigerator for 2 hours.

2 For the stew: Make a *bouquet garni* (herb bundle): set a large pot over medium heat. To the dry pot, add the lemongrass, cinnamon, star anise and bay leaves. Heat until fragrant, 2–4 minutes. Remove the spices and place them into a cheesecloth; wrap loosely and tie with butcher's twine to make a bouquet garni.

3 In the same large pot, heat the annatto oil over high heat until it shimmers. In batches, sear the marinated beef on all sides. Set the beef aside. Lower the heat to medium, add the onion and cook until translucent, scraping the bottom of the pan. Add the tomato paste, return the beef to the pot, and cook, stirring, for 5 minutes. Add the vegetable stock, coconut water, paprika and the prepared bouquet garni from step 2. Bring the liquid to a boil, lower to a simmer, cover and cook for 1 hour. Add the carrot, salt and soy sauce. Return to a simmer and cook uncovered until the carrot chunks are tender, about 30 minutes. Taste and add salt as needed. Spoon into bowls and garnish with the coriander leaves and Thai basil. Serve with warmed baguette.

Vegetarian options: Substitute a mix of your favorite fresh and dried mushrooms for the beef. Substitute 2 tablespoons tamari sauce and 2 tablespoons vegetarian oyster sauce for the fish sauce. Add 1 tablespoon of vegan butter to the stew.

Yield 4 Servings
Prep time: 4½ hours
    (includes marinating)
Cook time: 20–25 mins

For the pork:
½ cup (170 g) honey
4 cloves garlic, crushed
2 shallots, diced
2 lemongrass stalks,
    white parts, diced
2 teaspoons fish sauce
2 teaspoons annatto oil
2 teaspoons condensed milk
2 teaspoons toasted sesame oil
1 teaspoon sesame seeds, toasted
½ teaspoon dark soy sauce
1 teaspoon freshly ground black
    pepper
¾ lb (375 g) pork shoulder, thinly
    sliced
¾ lb (375 g) pork belly, thinly sliced

For the pickled vegetables:
½ cup (125 ml) hot water
¼ cup (50 g) sugar
½ cup (125 ml) rice wine vinegar
1½ cups (205 g) shredded cucumbers
1½ cups (135 g) shredded carrots

To serve:
8 oz (225 g) dried rice noodles
½ cup (10 g) coarsely chopped mint
½ cup (10 g) coarsely chopped
    coriander leaves (cilantro)
½ cup (10 g) coarsely chopped
    Thai basil leaves
½ cup (10 g) coarsely
    chopped culantro
½ cup (10 g) perilla leaves
½ cup (70 g) chopped peanuts
2 limes, cut into wedges
Dipping Sauce (see page 31)

Rice Noodles with Barbecue
Bún Thịt Nướng

Most Vietnamese recipes include a lot of ingredients, and it's well worth it to include them all: the result is unmatched depth and flavor. Every food is new to us at some point in our lives, and I hope the ingredients that are new to you in these recipes will become staples in your home one day.

1 For the pork: In a large bowl, whisk together the honey, garlic, shallot, lemongrass, fish sauce, annatto oil, condensed milk, sesame oil, sesame seeds, dark soy sauce and black pepper. Add the pork, toss to coat well, cover, and marinate for 4 hours in the refrigerator.

2 For the pickled vegetables: add the hot water and sugar to a bowl and mix until the sugar is dissolved. Add the rice vinegar and stir to combine. Add the cucumber and carrot and set aside for 1 hour. Drain and discard the liquid.

3 To serve: Meanwhile, cook the rice noodles according to package instructions; drain and rinse with cold water.

4 Preheat a grill to medium-low. Using a non-stick vegetable or fish grill basket/pan, grill the pork over indirect heat until cooked thoroughly.

5 Add the noodles, herbs, carrot, cucumber, peanuts and lime wedges to individual serving bowls. Divide the grilled pork among the 4 bowls and serve with Dipping Sauce on the side.

Vegetarian options: Substitute tempeh for pork. Eliminate fish sauce in the marinade; substitute with 1½ teaspoons crushed pineapple and 1½ teaspoons soy sauce.

Spicy Hue Style Noodle Soup
Bún Bò Huế

Makes 8 Servings
Prep time: 20 mins
Cook time: 2–3 hours

For the broth:
1 tablespoon annatto oil
2 shallots, minced
8 cloves garlic, minced
1½ lbs (725 g) beef brisket, thinly sliced
2 lbs (900 g) oxtail
1½ lbs (680 g) pork belly, thinly sliced
2¾ cups (700 ml) high quality chicken stock
4 cups (1 liter) high quality pork broth
8 lemongrass stalks, smashed
Water, as needed
1 tablespoon salt
2 teaspoons sugar
2 teaspoons shrimp paste
1 tablespoon fish sauce

This recipe traditionally calls for congealed pork blood, but because it is difficult to ensure the correct flavor and consistency, I have omitted it. If you have access to fresh pork blood, however, consider using it: adding it to this recipe would be a tribute to its authenticity.

The soup gets its name from its place of origin, the city of Huế. Bún Bò Huế is one of the three most popular soups in Vietnam, and its ingredients vary dramatically throughout the country. Common ingredients include pork knuckles and the aforementioned congealed pig blood. What makes this soup so delicious is its combination of spiciness and saltiness with the lemongrass flavor.

1 For the broth: In a large pot, heat the annatto oil over medium heat until shimmering. Sauté the shallot and garlic until fragrant. Add the brisket, oxtail, pork belly, stock, broth and lemongrass. Add enough water to just cover the meat, raise the heat to high, and bring the liquid to a boil. Reduce to medium-high to maintain a steady simmer and add the salt,

To serve:

1 lb (500 g) dried thick rice
   noodles

1 bunch Thai basil

1 tablespoon annatto
   flakes

1 bird's eye chili pepper,
   thinly sliced

2 limes, cut into wedges

sugar and shrimp paste. Cook uncovered, adding more water as needed. After about 1 hour, check the pork for doneness, and remove it when it reaches 145°F (63°C). The brisket and oxtail will need 2–3 hours. Once the meat easily falls off the bone, remove and set aside with the pork. Remove and discard the lemongrass from the broth, add the fish sauce, and let the broth simmer for another 20 minutes.

2 To serve: Meanwhile, prepare the rice noodles according to the package instructions. Drain and rinse with cold water.

3 Place the noodles and meat into individual bowls and spoon the warm broth over top. Garnish each bowl with basil leaves, annatto flakes, chili pepper and lime wedges.

Main Dishes   **113**

Rice Vermicelli with Chicken, Shrimp & Ham

Bún Thang

Makes 6–8 Servings
Prep time: 20 mins
Cook time: 20–25 mins

2½ lbs (1.25 kg) bone-in skin-on chicken thighs and breasts
1 yellow onion, halved
⅓ cup (33 g) dried baby shrimp
3 cups (750 ml) high quality vegetable broth
Water, as needed
1¼ teaspoons fish sauce
Salt, to taste
1 lb (500 g) dried rice noodles (vermicelli)
6 large eggs, lightly beaten
¾ lb (350 g) Vietnamese ham, sliced (optionally substitute mortadella, pork sausage or tofu)
½ bunch culantro, whole
6 green onions (scallions), thinly sliced
1 bird's eye chili pepper, seeds removed, thinly sliced

The word *bun* means "noodle," and *thang* refers to soup. The broth that forms the base of this dish, which hails from Hanoi, is as simple as its name indicates: noodle soup. What differentiates this chicken soup from other soups, like *phở ga*, is the addition of shrimp and Vietnamese ham.

1 Add the chicken, onion, dried shrimp and vegetable broth to a large pot. Add enough water to cover the chicken by about 1 inch (2.5 cm). Bring the liquid to a boil, and then reduce to a simmer and cook until the chicken is cooked through, about 20 minutes. Remove the chicken from the liquid and set aside to cool; remove and discard the onion. Shred the chicken meat and discard the bones. Add the fish sauce to the broth, along with salt, as needed. Return the shredded chicken to the broth and simmer for another 5 minutes.

2 Meanwhile, prepare the rice noodles according to the package instructions. Drain and rinse with cold water.

3 Set a non-stick pan over medium heat. Add just enough beaten egg to thinly coat the pan. Cook until set on both sides, flipping about halfway through cooking. Remove from the pan and roll into a cigar shape. Repeat with the remaining egg. Once all the egg is cooked and rolled, thinly slice the cigar rolls into ribbons.

4 Divide the noodles between bowls. Top with the ham, egg, herbs and chili pepper. Top each bowl with hot broth, evenly portioning the chicken and shrimp. Serve hot.

Makes 6 Servings

Prep time: 1 hour (includes soaking and chilling)

Cook time: 2 hours

For the meatballs:

1½ lbs (750 g) ground pork

6 dried wood ear mushrooms, soaked in cold water for 2 hours, drained, and diced

¼ cup (35 g) minced shallots

2 teaspoons fish sauce

2 teaspoons oyster sauce

1 teaspoon sugar

1 teaspoon salt

1 teaspoon ground white pepper

For the broth:

3 lbs (1.5 kg) pork ribs

2 cups (500 ml) high quality pork stock

2 cups (500 ml) high quality mushroom broth

3 teaspoons minced garlic

2 large yellow onions, halved

1 bunch green onions (scallions), thinly sliced

1 teaspoon freshly ground black pepper

3-in (7.5-cm) piece fresh ginger, peeled and thinly sliced

Water, as needed

1½ cups (60 g) dried shiitake mushrooms, soaked in water for 20 minutes, drained, and sliced

Salt, to taste

To serve:

12 oz (350 g) dried rice noodles (vermicelli)

1 bird's eye chili pepper, thinly sliced

Pork & Mushroom Noodle Soup

Bún Mọc

This dish was created in Thanh Xuân, the district where I've lived the longest in Vietnam. I spent many nights in my neighbors' homes cooking and eating *bún mọc* because it's honest good food, and cooking inevitably brings friends closer together.

1 For the meatballs: In a large mixing bowl, combine the pork, wood ear mushroom, shallot, fish sauce, oyster sauce, sugar, salt and white pepper. Mix to combine well and shape into small meatballs with your hands. Refrigerate the meatballs for at least 30 minutes.

2 For the broth: Meanwhile, place the pork ribs, stock, broth, garlic, onion, green onion, black pepper and ginger in a large pot. Add enough water to cover the pork ribs by about 1 inch (2.5 cm). Bring to a boil, reduce to a simmer, and cook uncovered for 1½ hours, skimming the top and adding water as needed. Remove the pork ribs from the pot to cool slightly. Debone the ribs in chunks, discarding the bones. Place the pork rib meat, along with the meatballs and shiitake mushroom into the pot. Simmer for 30 more minutes, until the meatballs are cooked through and the mushroom slices are tender. Taste and add salt as needed.

3 To serve: Meanwhile, prepare the rice noodles according to the package instructions. Drain and rinse with cold water.

4 Divide the noodles into individual serving bowls. Top with the hot broth and a serving of the rib meat, meatballs and mushrooms. Top with the chili pepper.

Fried Chicken with Salted Egg Sauce
Gà Sốt Trứng Muối

Makes 4 Servings
Prep time: 20 mins
Cook time: 15–20 mins

For the chicken:
½ cup (70 g) all-purpose flour
½ cup (70 g) cornstarch
1 teaspoon salt
1 teaspoon freshly ground black pepper
1 egg
1 lb (500 g) boneless chicken thighs, cubed
Oil for frying

For the sauce:
4 salted duck egg yolks
1 tablespoon butter
2 teaspoons minced garlic
2 bird's eye chili peppers, seeds removed, thinly sliced
1 teaspoon sugar
12 Vietnamese basil leaves
2 teaspoons vegetable oil

To serve:
6 cups (1.5 kg) cooked white rice
2 limes, cut into wedges

If I find salted egg as a feature of *anything* on a menu in Vietnam, I guarantee the dish will be delicious. Salted egg can steal the show in any recipe—this one included.

1 For the chicken: In a shallow bowl, mix the flour, cornstarch, salt and pepper. In a separate bowl, beat the egg. Coat the chicken pieces in the egg, followed by the flour mixture. Heat the oil in a medium skillet on medium-high until shimmering. Fry the chicken in small batches until golden brown and cooked through, about 3–4 minutes per batch.

2 For the sauce: Place the egg yolks in a heat-proof bowl atop a rack in a large pot with 1 inch (2.5 cm) of boiling water. Cover and steam the egg yolks for 5–10 minutes; their consistency should start to thicken, but not become firm. Mash the yolks and set aside. In a medium skillet, melt the butter on low heat. Add the yolks and cook, stirring, until bubbles appear. Add the chili pepper, sugar and Vietnamese basil and cook for another 1–2 minutes, stirring constantly. Add the chicken and toss until coated. Remove from the heat. Serve warm over rice and garnish with lime wedges.

Makes 8 Servings

Prep time: 30–35 mins
(includes soaking)

Cook time: 15–20 mins

For the squid:
½ cup (125 ml) annatto oil
8 oz (250 g) dried squid,
soaked in cold water for
20 minutes and drained
1 teaspoon oyster sauce
1 teaspoon sugar

For the prawns and pork belly:
½ cup (20 g) dried prawns, soaked
in water for 1 hour
8 oz (227 g) skinless pork belly, cut
into cubes
1 clove garlic, minced
4 teaspoons sliced green onions
(scallions)
1 teaspoon salt
1 teaspoon sugar
¼ teaspoon ground white pepper
1½ teaspoons soy sauce

To assemble:
10 oz (330 g) rice paper sheets,
cut into thin strips
2 teaspoons tamarind sauce
1 teaspoon oyster sauce
Green Onion Oil (see page 31)
8 oz (250 g) high quality sweet beef
jerky, cut into 1-in (2.5-cm) slices
2 green mangoes, cut into thin
matchsticks
⅔ cup (90 g) roasted peanuts,
crushed
2 teaspoons shrimp salt, plus more,
to taste
10 hard boiled eggs, quartered
1 cup (60 g) fried shallot

Rice Paper Mixed Noodles
Bánh Tráng Trộn

This favorite was originally a "leftover special," composed of the remainders of other dishes. These days, however, it's more like a gourmet salad.

1 For the squid: Heat the oil in a large skillet over high heat until shimmering. Add the squid and fry for 30 seconds. Using a slotted spoon or tongs, transfer the squid to a paper towel-lined plate (reserve the frying oil for the shrimp). Once the squid has cooled, use scissors and your hands to shred the squid into long, thin strips. In another non-stick skillet over medium heat, cook the squid, oyster sauce and sugar until the squid is crispy.

2 For the prawns and pork belly: Drain the prawns and pat dry with paper towels to remove excess moisture. Add the prawns and pork belly to a food processor and pulse until finely ground. In a bowl, combine the ground prawn and pork belly mixture with the garlic, green onions, salt, sugar, white pepper and soy sauce. Heat the reserved frying oil until shimmering. Add the ground prawn and pork belly mixture to the skillet. Cook, stirring, until golden and crispy, about 1 minute. Use a slotted spoon to remove the mixture from the oil and transfer to paper towels to drain.

3 To assemble: In a large bowl, combine the rice paper strips, tamarind sauce, oyster sauce and one teaspoon of the Green Onion Oil. Coat the rice paper strips completely, adding more tamarind sauce, oyster sauce and Green Onion Oil as needed.

4 Add the squid, prawn and pork belly, beef jerky, mango, peanut and shrimp salt. Lightly drizzle with Green Onion Oil. Add more shrimp salt, as needed. Top with the egg quarters and fried shallot, and serve with the remaining Green Onion Oil on the side.

Lemongrass Chicken with Rice Noodles
Bún Gà Nướng

Makes 4 servings
Prep time: 2–4 hours
   (includes marinating)
Cook time: 20–25 mins

For the dipping sauce:
¼ cup (60 ml) fresh lime
   juice
¼ cup (65 ml) water
2 tablespoons fish sauce
2 tablespoons honey
1 teaspoon sweet
   chili sauce

For the chicken:
2 lemongrass stalks (white
   parts only), smashed
3 cloves garlic, minced
3 tablespoons fresh
   lime juice
2 tablespoons fish sauce
1 tablespoon soy sauce
2 tablespoons brown sugar
1 shallot, peeled
   and halved
2 tablespoons vegetable
   oil, divided
1½ lbs (750 g) boneless
   chicken thighs
8 oz (250 g) dried rice
   noodles (vermicelli)

Over the years, I've cooked this dish using chicken thighs, legs, wings and even necks. This recipe specifies boneless thighs, but feel free to prepare it with your preferred cut—it won't impact the taste.

1 For the dipping sauce: In a small bowl, combine the lime juice, water, fish sauce, honey and sweet chili sauce. Set aside.

2 For the chicken: In a shallow bowl, mix the lemongrass, garlic, lime juice, fish sauce, soy sauce, brown sugar, shallot and 1 tablespoon of the vegetable oil. Add the chicken thighs and toss until thoroughly coated. Cover and refrigerate for 2–4 hours.

3 Prepare the rice noodles according to the package instructions. Drain, rinse with cold water, and set aside.

4 Warm the remaining tablespoon of oil in a large skillet over medium heat until shimmering. Remove the chicken from the marinade, add it to the pan, and cook until golden brown on both sides and cooked through, about 6–8 minutes per side. Remove from the heat and set aside to rest for 5 minutes. Slice into thin pieces.

5 Serve the chicken with the room-temperature noodles and dipping sauce on the side.

Lemongrass Tofu
Đậu Hũ Sả

Makes 4 servings
Prep time: 35–40 mins
    (includes marinating)
Cook time: 10–15 mins

2 lemongrass stalks,
    minced
2 teaspoons honey
1 tablespoon soy sauce
1 bird's eye chili pepper,
    thinly sliced
½ teaspoon ground
    turmeric
Pinch of salt
1 lb (500 g) firm tofu, cut
    into 1½-in (3.75-cm)
    squares
2 tablespoons vegetable
    oil, divided
1 shallot, minced
3 cloves garlic, minced
1 bunch green onions
    (scallions), thinly sliced
¼ cup (35 g) chopped
    peanuts
2 cups (500 g) cooked
    white rice

It's reassuring to know that any time I don't feel like making my own fresh tofu, I'm always able to find some in the mornings in the wet markets of Hanoi. The flavor of fresh tofu is much more memorable.

1 In a large bowl, combine the lemongrass, honey, soy sauce, chili pepper, turmeric and salt. Mix well, add the tofu, and toss until thoroughly coated. Cover and set aside to marinate for 30 minutes.

2 In a large skillet set over medium heat, warm 1 tablespoon of the vegetable oil until shimmering. Add the tofu and cook, turning frequently, until all sides are cooked evenly, 5–8 minutes. Transfer to a plate and set aside.

3 Return the pan to the heat and add the remaining 1 tablespoon vegetable oil. Sauté the shallot until translucent. Add the garlic and green onions, and stir until fragrant. Return the tofu to the pan, mix well, and cook for another 2 minutes, making sure the garlic doesn't burn. Remove from the heat.

4 Top with the peanuts and serve with steamed rice or rice noodles.

Shrimp & Pork Rice Dumplings

Bánh Bột Lọc

Makes 6 Servings
Prep time: 40–45 mins
Cook time: 20–25 mins

For the dough:
⅔ cup (120 g) potato starch, plus more as needed
1½ cups (180 g) wheat starch
¼ teaspoon salt
½ cup (125 ml) room temperature water
2 cups (500 ml) boiling water
1 teaspoon vegetable oil

For the filling:
4–8 oz (100–250 g) small shrimp (51/60), peeled and diced
8 oz (250 g) ground pork (80/20)
1 teaspoon salt
½ teaspoon white pepper
1 teaspoon sugar
1 teaspoon oyster sauce
1 tablespoon vegetable oil

To serve:
Dipping Sauce (see page 31)
Thinly sliced green onions (scallions) (optional)
Fried shallot (optional)

This recipe supposedly yields 6 servings, but I can make a batch all for myself and snack on the dumplings all day! They're also great with pork belly instead of ground pork.

1 For the dough: In a large bowl, sift together the potato starch, wheat starch and salt. Add the room temperature and boiling water and mix thoroughly. Add extra potato starch, if needed, to thicken the dough so that it is manageable. Add the vegetable oil and combine with a spoon until the dough is cool enough to knead with your hands. Knead into a smooth ball, cover with a dish towel, and set aside.

2 For the filling: Combine the shrimp, pork, salt, pepper, sugar and oyster sauce. Heat the oil in a skillet until it shimmers. Add the filling mixture to the pan and cook, stirring occasionally, until the pork is cooked through.

3 To complete: Pull off pieces of the dough, ⅓–½ ounce (12–15 g) in weight. Roll each piece into a ball and flatten with your hand to desired size. Evenly distribute the filling in the center of each dumpling. Fold them in half. Seal the seam firmly by pinching it closed with your fingers or a fork.

4 Bring a large pot of water to a slow boil. Gently lower the dumplings into the water with a slotted spoon. Cook until the dumplings start to become transparent and float, about 10 minutes. Serve warm as a side or a main dish. Spoon the Dipping Sauce over the dumplings and garnish with green onion and fried shallot, if using.

Caramelized Catfish
Cá Kho Tộw

Makes 4 Servings
Prep time: 10 mins
Cook time: 10–15 mins

½ cup (100 g) brown sugar
Water, as needed
2 tablespoons fish sauce
1 tablespoon soy sauce
1 teaspoon peeled and
    grated fresh ginger
Four 6-oz (175-g)
    catfish fillets, skin on
    (optionally substitute
    any mild, flaky white
    fish)
1 lime, juiced
1 bird's eye chili pepper,
    seeded, thinly sliced
¼ cup (5 g) coarsely
    chopped fresh
    Thai basil

This rich, salty dish pairs perfectly with plain white rice. Warm memories of its complex and delicious flavors will have you searching for this dish every time you visit Vietnam.

1 Warm a large, heavy-bottomed pan over medium heat. Add the brown sugar with a tablespoon of water and cook, stirring and slowly adding more water as needed, until the sugar is dissolved and syrupy. Stir in the fish sauce, soy sauce and ginger. Bring the mixture to a simmer and cook until it turns a dark amber color.

2 Place the fish fillets into the pan skin-side down. Baste the fillets in the sauce and cover the pan with a lid. Allow to simmer until the fish is cooked through, 4–5 minutes. Remove from the heat.

3 Transfer the fish to a serving plate. Pour the remaining sauce over the fish. Drizzle with the lime juice and top with the chili pepper and Thai basil. Serve with rice.

Crispy Pan-Fried Trout
Chả Cá

Makes 2 Servings
Prep time: 20 mins
Cook time: 10–15 mins

1½ lbs (750 g) whole trout, scaled and gutted
1 teaspoon salt
1 teaspoon freshly ground black pepper
1 teaspoon mushroom powder
5 tablespoons vegetable oil, divided
¼ cup (30 g) cornstarch
2 cloves garlic, minced
3 tablespoons rice vinegar
2 tablespoons soy sauce
2 tablespoons sugar
1 tablespoon fish sauce
1 tablespoon oyster sauce
⅓ cup (10 g) coarsely chopped fresh coriander leaves (cilantro), for garnish

As I dined one day in the Mekong Delta region, a young man rode a bicycle up to the table, arm extended, to deliver my dinner—this delightful, pan-fried trout. There's nothing I enjoy more than being transported back to vivid memories as I enjoy a dish.

1 Pat the fish dry. Cut deep diagonal slits through the skin on both sides. Sprinkle the salt, black pepper and mushroom powder on both sides of the fish. Set aside for 15 minutes.

2 Add 3 tablespoons of the vegetable oil to a large, shallow pan and set over medium-high heat until shimmering. Quickly dredge the fish in the cornstarch, shaking off any excess, and carefully add the fish to the pan. Fry for about 3 minutes on each side until golden and cooked through. Remove from the heat and transfer to a paper towel-lined plate to drain.

3 In a small saucepan over medium heat, warm the remaining 2 tablespoons of oil and the garlic until fragrant. Add the rice vinegar, soy sauce, sugar, fish sauce, and oyster sauce and simmer, stirring, until the sugar is dissolved and the sauce is slightly thickened. Remove from the heat.

4 Garnish the fish with the coriander leaves and serve immediately with the sauce on the side.

Drinks and Desserts

When eating fruit, remember who planted the tree;
when drinking clear water, remember who dug the well.

—VIETNAMESE PROVERB

Drinks and Desserts

Travel brings myths alive

Hanoi's Hoàn Kiếm Lake or "Returned Sword Lake," is home to turtles, both real and legendary. Long ago, King Lê Lợi was said to have successfully fought off the Chinese army with the help of a magic sword. Afterward, as the king glided along in his boat, a giant, golden turtle emerged and absconded with the blade—and it was never seen again. Today, some people report that they've caught a glimpse of this magical beast. Luck is bestowed on those who do.

Travel lets hobbies take flight

In Vietnam, there's a flourishing bird club culture. Bird owners and their prized fowl gather throughout the country in early morning rituals and competitions. This is nothing like dog clubs (think Westminster) in other places. Bird culture is ever-present throughout the country, and many indulge in this hobby.

Which beautiful creature can sing the loudest, the longest, the most exquisitely?

Travel makes the anxious calm (even while caffeinated)

In Vietnam, drinking tea is as important as drinking water. The practice of "tea meditation" is believed to have begun

◀ **A variety of colorful shaved-ice dessert toppings on offer in a restaurant.**

in Buddhist temples and served as the introduction of tea into everyday life.

According to legend, a French Catholic priest introduced coffee to Vietnam in 1857. Today, Vietnam is the second largest exporter of coffee in the world. Vietnamese coffee, a thicker, richer, more acidic and highly caffeinated version of espresso, is traditionally drip-brewed using a *phin*, a small metal chamber that fits atop a coffee cup. Sweetened condensed milk is added to help cut the bitterness. I can promise that you'll never have a bad cup of coffee in Vietnam.

The pleasing fragrance of travel

Just thirty minutes outside of Hanoi, you'll find "Incense Village," the nickname of the area where most of the incense made in Vietnam is crafted. No matter what belief system or religion one follows, the traditional Vietnamese ritual of burning incense symbolizes the bridging of the gap between life and death to the Vietnamese people. An alternate connotation is that the incense's fragrance spreading far and wide symbolizing the spread of good deeds throughout the world.

Egg Coffee
Cà Phê Trứng

Makes 4 Cups
Prep time: 5 mins
Cook time: 5 mins

2 oz (50 g) Vietnamese
   coffee, finely ground
4 cups (1 liter) hot water
2 egg yolks
½ cup (125 ml) sweetened
   condensed milk
1 teaspoon vanilla extract

The beverage that epitomizes Vietnam is egg coffee. Originally created in Hanoi, this drink layers sweet, creamy, and frothy egg yolk beaten with sweetened condensed milk on top and strong Vietnamese coffee on the bottom. It's coffee and dessert combined in a single glass. When you visit Hanoi, definitely try the egg coffee at Giang Café or Dinh Café!

1 Brew the coffee with the hot water according to your preferred method.

2 Meanwhile, whip the egg yolks, sweetened condensed milk, and vanilla extract to soft peaks.

3 To serve, divide the hot coffee between four cups and top each cup with the egg foam.

Sweet Corn Pudding with Coconut Cream
Chè Bắp

Makes 8 Servings
Prep time: 15–20 mins
Cook time: 1 hour, 30 mins

For the pudding:
4 ears sweet summer corn
4 cups (1 liter) water
2 cups (500 ml) high
    quality vegetable stock
½ cup (100 g) glutinous
    rice
4 teaspoons sugar
Pinch of salt

For the coconut sauce:
1¾ cups (425 ml) coconut
    milk
¼ teaspoon salt
2 teaspoons sugar
½ teaspoon vanilla
1 teaspoon cornstarch
    dissolved in 2
    teaspoons water
    (slurry)

To serve:
2 teaspoons sesame seeds,
    toasted

I spontaneously fall in love with some foods, and this is one of them. My introduction came during a stay with a family in the northern mountains. I watched the family pick the corn in their fields and cook the dish over an open fire to make the pudding. It was fresh and delicious!

1 For the pudding: Remove the kernels from the corn, reserving both the kernels and the cobs. Place the cobs in a pot with the water and stock. Bring to a boil, cover, reduce to a simmer, and cook for 1 hour. Remove and discard the corn cobs. Bring the liquid back to a boil. Add the rice, cover, reduce to a simmer, and cook until the rice has absorbed most of the water (15–20 minutes). Add the corn kernels, sugar and salt to the pot. Stir to combine. Return to a boil, and then reduce to a simmer and cook until the corn is tender, about 15 minutes. Taste and adjust the sugar and salt, if desired. Set aside.

2 For the coconut sauce: In a small saucepan, combine the coconut milk, salt, sugar and vanilla. Bring the mixture to a boil while stirring constantly. Add the slurry to the sauce, and then reduce to a simmer, continuing to stir, until the mixture thickens slightly. Remove from the heat.

3 Ladle the pudding into individual bowls. Serve warm or cold. Top with the sauce and toasted sesame seeds.

Tofu Pudding with Ginger Syrup
Tàu Hũ Nóng

Makes 6 Servings
Prep time: 10–15 mins
   (plus chilling overnight)
Cook time: 10–15 mins

For the tofu pudding:
4 cups (1 liter)
   unsweetened soy milk,
   divided
2 teaspoons sugar
1 teaspoon gelatin
½ teaspoon vanilla extract

For the ginger syrup:
3-in (7.5-cm) piece fresh
   ginger, peeled and
   thinly sliced
2 cups (500 ml) water
1 cup (215 g) brown sugar

This simple-to-make, warm dessert might become your new favorite. In it, silken tofu pairs incredibly with warm ginger syrup. The first time I had this, it was sold to me by a vendor walking around on a beach in Southern Vietnam. At first, the warm ginger surprised me, as I anticipated something cold on the beach—but it was surprisingly refreshing!

1 For the tofu pudding: Pour three cups of the soy milk into a large bowl. In a medium saucepan, whisk together the remaining 1 cup of soy milk, sugar, gelatin and vanilla until dissolved. Set the mixture over medium-low heat, and bring it to a gentle boil while whisking constantly. Once the liquid comes to a gentle boil, transfer the heated soy milk mixture to the bowl with the remaining 3 cups of soy milk. Whisk well to remove any lumps. Remove any bubbles on the top with a spoon. Cover with plastic wrap and refrigerate overnight.

2 For the ginger syrup: In a saucepan, set the ginger, water and brown sugar over medium heat. Stir until the sugar dissolves. Reduce to a simmer and cook until slightly thickened, about 5 minutes. Remove and discard the pieces of ginger. Set the syrup aside.

3 To serve: Using a large spoon, scoop out portions of the tofu pudding into bowls. Top with a generous amount of warm or chilled ginger syrup.

Mango Margaritas
Cocktail Xoài

Makes 4 Margaritas
Prep time: 10–15 mins

For the chili-salt rims:
2 teaspoons chili powder
1 teaspoon sea salt
1 lime, cut into wedges

For the margaritas:
4 small mangoes, peeled, pitted, and cubed
¾ cup (185 ml) silver tequila
¼ cup (65 ml) Grand Marnier
4 limes, juiced
2 teaspoons agave nectar
1 cup (150 g) ice

Sip this refreshing tropical margarita while you're waiting for your simmering pot of phở to be ready. Prepare it with or without the chili-salt rim, but definitely keep the lime!

1 For the chili-salt rims: On a small plate, mix the chili powder and salt. Rub a lime wedge around the edge of your glasses and press the rim into the chili salt mixture.

2 For the margaritas: Place the mango, tequila, Grand Marnier, lime juice, agave nectar and ice in a blender, and blend until smooth.

3 Pour the margaritas into the prepared glasses and garnish with lime wedges or extra cubes of mango.

Grilled Bananas with Sweet Coconut Rice

Chuối Nếp Nướng

Makes 4 Servings
Prep time: 6–8 hours
   (includes soaking)
Cook time: 50–55 mins

For the sticky rice:
1 cup (250 ml) full fat
   coconut milk, divided
2 tablespoons sugar
2 cups (400 g) sticky rice
Water, as needed
Pinch of salt
2 pandan leaves

**For the bananas and
   assembly:**
4 large bananas
1 tablespoon sugar
4–8 pandan leaves,
   depending on size of
   the bananas

For the coconut sauce:
1¼ cups (300 ml)
   coconut milk
1 teaspoon sugar
1 teaspoon cornstarch
¼ teaspoon salt

To serve:
Sesame seeds, toasted

Bananas grow and thrive year-round in Vietnam's climate, so this sophisticated dessert is available in all four seasons. Once you try it, you'll understand why it's popular. We often forget how different foods taste from different countries, bananas are included in this thought. The Vietnamese bananas, or *chuối cau*, are smaller, rounder and plumper. They are fragrant and have a delicate flavor, and they are typically still very firm when used for cooking.

1 For the sticky rice: In a small saucepan, heat the coconut milk and the sugar until the sugar is dissolved. Set aside. Place the rice in a pot and cover with water by at least 3 inches (8 cm). Soak for 6–8 hours. Rinse the rice well and drain. Toss the soaked rice with a pinch of salt, cover, and steam with 2 pandan leaves until soft, 20–30 minutes. While still hot, add the coconut milk and sugar mixture to the rice and mix well. Steam for 2–3 more minutes. Transfer rice and leaves to bowl. Cover the bowl until the liquid is completely absorbed. Discard the leaves. Allow to cool until manageable.

2 For the bananas and assembly: Meanwhile, peel the bananas and place in a bowl. If using long bananas, cut them in half. Sprinkle with the sugar and toss to coat. Cover and refrigerate for about 30 minutes.

3 Lay a pandan leaf on a flat surface. Top with one portion of the rice. Spread the rice onto the leaf. The length of the rice should be the same as that of the banana. The width of the rice should allow the rice to wrap around the banana one time. Place a banana on top of

the rice. Roll the leaf around the banana, making sure the rice covers the entire the banana, except for the ends. Repeat with remaining leaves, rice and bananas.

4 For the coconut sauce: In a small saucepan, mix the coconut milk, sugar, cornstarch and salt. Place the saucepan over high heat and bring the sauce to a boil while stirring constantly. As soon as it comes to a boil, remove the saucepan from the heat. Continue to stir for 30 more seconds.

5 Preheat a grill to medium-low. Place all rolls, seam side down, onto the grill. Rotate every few minutes to ensure all sides are grilled evenly. Grill until the leaves are blackened and the outer layer of rice is crispy, about 20–25 minutes. Peel off the leaves from the rolls. Slice each roll into 1-inch (2.5-cm) pieces. Place in shallow bowls. Drizzle with coconut sauce and sprinkle toasted sesame seeds on top. Serve warm.

Sweet Mung Bean Soup
Chè Hoa Cau

Makes 4 Servings
Prep time: 8–10 hours
    (includes soaking)
Cook time: 30–35 mins

For the soup:
1 cup (200 g) dried
    split mung beans,
    soaked overnight
Pinch of salt
¾ cup (160 g) brown sugar
1 cup (120 g) tapioca
    starch
4 cups (1 liter) water
1 teaspoon grapefruit
    extract

For the sauce:
1¾ cups (420 ml) coconut
    milk
Dash of cardamom powder
⅛ teaspoon salt
1 teaspoon tapioca flour
    dissolved in 1 teaspoon
    water (slurry)
¼ cup (50 g) sugar
1 pandan leaf,
    cut into strips

The word *chè* is used to describe a wide range of desserts that hail from different regions of Vietnam, but they almost always share a common ingredient: coconut milk.

Mung bean soup, a popular and classic *chè* from northern Vietnam, is vegan, dairy free, and gluten free. It's the best kind of comfort food.

1 For the soup: Drain, and then steam the mung beans for 15 minutes or until soft. Add a pinch of salt. In a small saucepan over medium-high heat, whisk together the brown sugar, tapioca flour and water until the starch and sugar are dissolved. Turn to medium-low. Whisk over the heat for 3–4 more minutes. Remove from the heat and stir in the mung beans and grapefruit extract. Set aside.

2 For the sauce: In a small saucepan, whisk together the coconut milk, cardamom powder and salt. Simmer until it starts to steam. Reduce to low and add the tapioca flour slurry to the saucepan. Stirring constantly, heat until the sauce starts to thicken. Add the sugar and pandan leaf and continue to cook on low for an additional 2–3 minutes, or until it begins to thicken. Remove from the heat and remove the pandan leaf strips (they can be discarded or used as decorative garnish). Allow the sauce to cool slightly before serving.

3 Ladle the soup into serving bowls and top with the sauce. Serve room temperature or chilled.

Sweet Lotus Seed Soup
Chè Sen

Makes 4 Servings
Prep time: 10 mins
Cook time: 30–35 mins

12 oz (350 g) fresh lotus seeds, germs removed (optionally substitute with canned lotus seeds)
2 cups (500 ml) water
⅓ cup (65 g) rock sugar, plus more to taste
¼ teaspoon vanilla extract
Crushed ice (optional)

This sweet soup is made with the seeds of Vietnam's national flower, the lotus. You'll find it to be simple to make and absolutely delicious. After a lifetime of using canned lotus seeds for recipes prepared in the States, I now find it difficult to bring myself to use anything but fresh lotus seeds.

1 Steam the lotus seeds for 20–25 minutes until they start to soften. In a saucepan, bring the water to a boil. Add the steamed lotus seeds, reduce the heat to medium-low, and simmer until soft, about 10 minutes. Add the rock sugar and simmer just until the sugar is fully dissolved. Add the vanilla extract. Transfer the mixture to a bowl to cool.

2 Serve the soup room temperature or chilled. Top with crushed ice, if using.

Sticky Rice Pudding with Beans & Coconut Cream

Chè Đậu

Makes 4 Servings
Prep time: 3–4 hours
    (includes soaking)
Cook time: 1 hour, 10 mins

For the beans:
1 cup (170 g) dried black-
    eyed peas/beans
1 teaspoon baking soda

For the pudding:
1 cup (200 g) sweet
    glutinous rice, soaked
    overnight, drained, and
    rinsed
4 pandan leaves
⅓ cup (65 g) cane sugar
½ teaspoon salt
4 cups (1 liter) water
1 teaspoon tapioca flour
    dissolved in 1 teaspoon
    water (slurry)

**For the coconut cream
    sauce:**
1½ cups (375 ml) coconut
    cream
1 teaspoon sugar
1 teaspoon tapioca flour
½ teaspoon salt
⅛ teaspoon vanilla extract

To serve:
1 cup (80 g) toasted
    coconut pieces
    (optional)
1 cup (165 g) diced mango
    (optional)

This classic dessert is topped with a delicious coconut cream sauce that will have you going back for seconds.

1 For the beans: Soak the beans with the baking soda for three hours. Rinse the beans well in cold water and discard any loose outer shells. Bring a pot of water to a boil, add the beans, and cook until just tender, about 20 minutes. Set aside.

2 For the pudding: Add the rice, pandan leaves, sugar, salt and water to a pot. Bring to a boil. Reduce heat to medium-low, cover, and simmer until the water is absorbed, 20–25 minutes. Stir the cooked beans and tapioca slurry into the rice. Continue mixing as you add the slurry to avoid clumping. Simmer on low heat for 10 minutes or until it reaches your preferred consistency.

3 For the coconut cream sauce: Add the coconut cream, sugar, tapioca flour, salt and vanilla to a small saucepan. Bring the mixture to a boil, lower to a simmer, and stir until the sauce thickens slightly. Remove from the heat.

4 To serve: Ladle the warm pudding into bowls. Add toasted coconut and mango (if using). Top with coconut cream sauce.

Sticky Rice with Mango
Xôi Xoài

Makes 6 Servings
Prep time: 8–10 hours
(includes soaking)
Cook time: 35–45 mins

For the rice:
1 cup (250 ml) full fat coconut milk
⅓ cup (65 g) sugar
¼ teaspoon salt
1½ cups (300 g) sticky rice, soaked overnight

For the sauce:
⅓ cup (80 ml) full fat coconut milk
1 tablespoon sugar

To serve:
1 teaspoon sesame seeds, toasted (optional)
1 large mango, peeled, pitted, and cut into thin slices (at least 24)

Sticky rice with mango is popular in every country in Indochina, and for good reason. I could eat this dessert every day.

1 For the rice: In a small saucepan, bring 1 cup of the coconut milk to a boil with the sugar and salt, stirring until the sugar is dissolved. Set aside. Steam the rice, covered, for 25–40 minutes (until tender), stirring halfway through cooking. In a large bowl, combine the cooked rice and the coconut milk mixture. Let the rice stand, covered, until the liquid is absorbed, about 30 minutes.

2 For the sauce: In a small saucepan, bring the coconut milk and sugar to a slow boil, stirring occasionally, for 1 minute. Transfer the sauce to a small bowl and chill until cool and thickened slightly.

3 To serve: Scoop the rice into bowls. Drizzle with the sauce and sprinkle with sesame seeds, if using. Divide the mango slices among the plates.

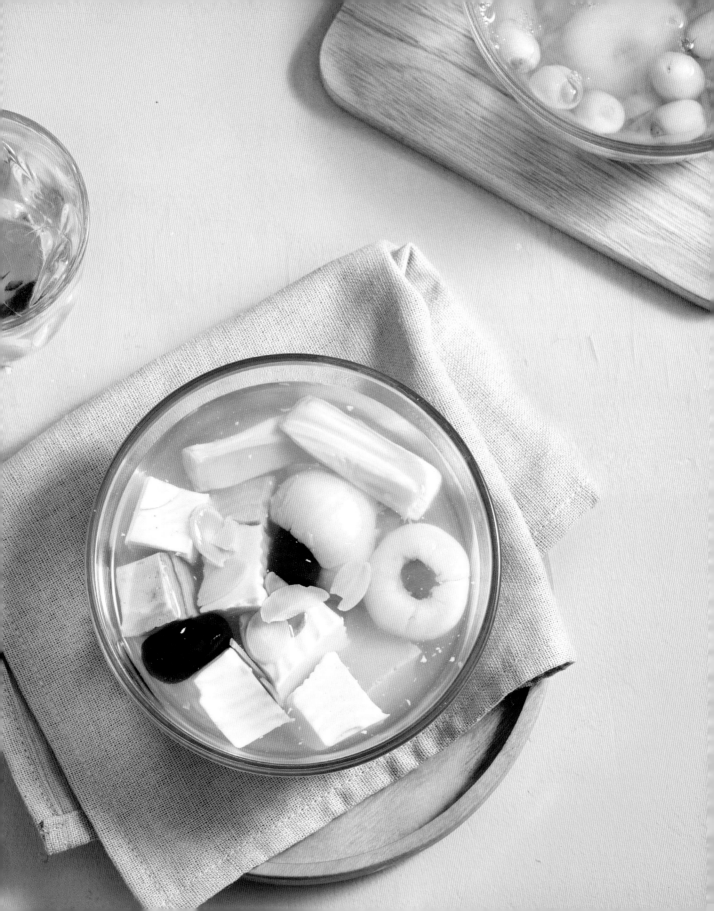

Sweet Mixed Soup
Chè Khúc Bạch

Makes 8 Servings
Prep time: 10 mins (plus
    chilling overnight)
Cook time: 15–20 mins

For the tofu pudding:
4 cups (1 liter)
    unsweetened soy milk,
    divided
2 teaspoons sugar
1 teaspoon gelatin powder
½ teaspoon vanilla extract

For the coconut sauce:
1¼ cups (300 ml) coconut
    cream
¼ cup (80 g) sweetened
    condensed coconut
    milk
¼ teaspoon salt

One 20-oz (570 g) can
    lychees, peeled
    and pitted
One 20-oz (570 g) can
    longans, peeled
    and pitted

To serve:
½ cup (60 g) sliced
    almonds, toasted
1 mango, peeled, pitted,
    and cut into strips
Shaved ice (optional)

The first time I tasted this dish was at a buffet restaurant in Hanoi. No one in our group ordered a beverage, but I didn't think anything of it. Later, I discovered their plan: instead of paying for a soda, they just drank the liquid from this sweet soup. Surprisingly, I now find myself partaking in this same ritual.

1 For the tofu pudding: Pour three cups of the soy milk into a deep pan and set aside. In a medium saucepan, whisk together the remaining 1 cup soy milk, sugar, gelatin and vanilla until dissolved. Set the mixture over medium-low heat and bring to a gentle boil while whisking constantly. Once the liquid comes to a gentle boil, transfer the heated soy milk mixture to the pan of remaining soy milk. Whisk well to remove any lumps. With a spoon, remove any bubbles on the surface. Cover with plastic wrap and refrigerate overnight.

2 For the coconut sauce: In a small saucepan, whisk together the coconut cream, condensed coconut milk and salt. Bring to a low boil over medium. Remove from the heat; let cool completely.

3 To serve: Drain the cans of lychees and longans, reserving the syrups. Evenly divide the lychees and longans between the serving bowls. Combine the syrups of both canned fruits and spoon 3 tablespoons over each bowl. Add 1 tablespoon of the coconut sauce to each bowl. While in the pan, cut the tofu pudding into 1-inch (2.5-cm) squares. Top each bowl with 3 or 4 cubes of tofu pudding, 1 tablespoon of toasted sliced almonds, slices of mango and shaved ice, if using.

Rice Balls in Ginger Syrup
Bánh Trôi Tàu

Makes 4 Servings
Prep time: 8–10 hours
   (includes soaking)
Cook time: 1 hour

For the ginger syrup:
One 2-in (5-cm) piece fresh
   ginger, peeled and
   thinly sliced
4 oz (100 g) palm sugar
1½ cups (375 ml) water

**For the mung bean
   filling:**
½ cup (100 g) dried split
   mung beans (soaked
   overnight)
1 tablespoon coconut milk
1 teaspoon sugar
⅛ teaspoon salt
1 teaspoon sesame oil

For the glutinous dough:
1 cup (140 g) glutinous
   rice flour, plus more as
   needed
1 cup (240 ml) warm water
⅛ teaspoon salt

Bánh trôi tàu is an indispensable part of Vietnamese culture. The best way I can describe it? Scrumptious pops of flavor in a warm ginger bath. There are certain flavors that I will always associate with Vietnamese cooking, and ginger is one of them.

1 For the ginger syrup: In a small saucepan, place the ginger, palm sugar and water over medium heat. Stir until the sugar dissolves. Reduce the heat to a simmer and cook for 30 minutes. Remove and discard the ginger from the syrup.

2 For the mung bean filling: Drain, and then steam the mung beans for 15 minutes or until soft. Add the steamed mung beans, coconut milk, sugar, salt and sesame oil to a food processor. Blend until smooth. Transfer to the refrigerator until cool enough to handle. Scoop scant tablespoons of the paste and form them into balls. Place the balls on a cookie sheet, cover with plastic wrap, and refrigerate.

3 For the glutinous dough: Sift the flour into a medium bowl. Add the warm water, while stirring continuously, until the mixture is firm. If needed, add more flour so the dough isn't sticky. Cover with a damp towel. Set aside to rest for 20 minutes.

4 For the coconut sauce: In a small saucepan over medium heat, combine the coconut cream, sugar, pandan leaf and salt. Stir to combine and cook until the mixture starts to bubble. Remove from the heat, discard the pandan leaf, and set aside.

For the coconut sauce:
¾ cup (185 ml) coconut
    cream
2 teaspoons sugar
1 pandan leaf
⅛ teaspoon salt

To serve:
1 teaspoon toasted
    sesame seeds

5 Shape the dough into balls larger than the mung bean filling balls. Flatten each dough ball into a round disc. Place a ball of mung bean filling in the center and wrap the dough around it, forming a ball that completely covers the mung bean filling. Roll the ball between your palms to make it smooth. Repeat with the remaining dough and mung bean balls.

6 Meanwhile, bring a large pot of water to a boil. Add the rice balls, gently stirring to prevent sticking at the bottom of the pot. Simmer until the surfaces of the dough balls are almost translucent, about 8–10 minutes. In batches, remove the rice balls with a slotted spoon and transfer them to the saucepan with the ginger syrup. Simmer for 5 minutes. Divide the rice balls and ginger syrup among serving bowls. Top with coconut sauce and toasted sesame seeds. Serve warm.

Taro Pudding with Coconut Cream
Chè Khoai Dẻo

Makes 4 Servings
Prep time: 8½ hours
    (includes soaking)
Cook time: 30 mins

For the coconut sauce:
1 cup (250 ml) coconut
    milk
⅓ cup (80 ml) water
¼ cup (50 g) sugar
½ teaspoon cornstarch
⅛ teaspoon salt

For the pudding:
2½ cups (625 ml) water
¾ lb (350 g) taro root,
    peeled and cut
    into cubes
½ cup (100 g) sweet
    glutinous rice, rinsed
½ cup (100 g) sugar
½ cup (125 ml) coconut
    milk
⅛ teaspoon salt

This recipe is a wonderful blend of traditional Vietnamese flavors. Although its ingredients may differ slightly depending on where you are in Vietnam, taro pudding, hearty and sweet, is always the main ingredient of *chè khoai dẻo*.

1 For the coconut sauce: In a small saucepan, mix together the coconut milk, water, sugar, cornstarch and salt. Bring the mixture to a boil, remove from the heat, and set aside.

2 For the pudding: In a medium pot, bring the water to a boil. Add the taro and rice, and return the mixture to a boil. Cover and simmer over medium-low heat for 15 minutes, stirring occasionally to prevent sticking at the bottom. Once the taro and rice are soft, add the sugar, coconut milk and salt. Bring the mixture back to a boil over medium heat. Remove from the heat.

3 Divide the pudding into individual bowls and top with coconut sauce. Serve warm or cold.

Vietnamese Layer Cake

Bánh Da Lợn

Makes 8–10 Servings
Prep time: 9 hours
(includes soaking)
Cook time: 45 mins

For the mung bean (yellow) layer:
½ cup (100 g) dried, split mung beans, soaked overnight
⅛ teaspoon salt
1¾ cups (425 ml) water
¾ cup (90 g) tapioca flour
2 teaspoons rice flour
½ cup (100 g) sugar
½ cup (125 ml) coconut milk
½ teaspoon vanilla extract
2 drops yellow food coloring

For the pandan (green) layer:
1½ cups (180 g) tapioca flour
¼ cup (35 g) rice flour
½ cup (100 g) sugar
¼ teaspoon salt
1¾ cups (425 ml) water
¼ cup (65 ml) coconut milk
¼ teaspoon pandan extract ("paste")
2 drops green food coloring
Vegetable oil, for greasing

With its stunningly beautiful layers of green and yellow, this dessert will break the ice around any table—when you bring another culture into your home, it always stimulates great conversations.

Pandan is a tropical plant also known as "screwpine." It features a grassy flavor with notes of vanilla and coconut.

1 For the mung bean (yellow) layer: Drain, and then steam the mung beans until soft, about 15 minutes. Add the mung beans and salt to a food processor and process until smooth. Add the water, tapioca flour, rice flour, sugar, coconut milk, vanilla and food coloring. Mix on high until smooth. Divide the batter in half.

2 For the pandan (green) layer: sift together the tapioca flour, rice flour, sugar and salt. Add the water and coconut milk and whisk until smooth. Add the pandan extract and food coloring and stir to combine well. Divide the batter in half.

3 Coat two 9-inch (23-cm) square cake pans with oil. Bring a steamer to a boil. Reduce the heat to low. Warm the oiled, empty pan in the steamer for 4–5 minutes until hot.

4 For the first layer: Stir the green batter. Pour half of the first batch of green batter into the cake pan. Cover and steam for 5–8 minutes or until solidified. For the second layer: Stir the one batch of yellow batter and pour all of it atop the solidified green layer. Cover and steam for 8–10 minutes or until solidified. For the third layer: pour the remaining green batter from the first batch on top of the yellow layer. Cover and steam for 10–15 minutes, or until whole cake is solidified. Let cool for 1 hour. Repeat with the second pan. Once cool, cut the cakes with an oiled knife. Serve at room temperature or chilled.

Coconut Cream Martinis

Makes 2 Martinis
Prep time: 10 mins

For the coconut rims:
Honey
Coconut flakes

For the martinis:
¼ cup (65 ml) coconut rum
¼ cup (65 ml) vodka
¼ cup (65 ml) coconut
   cream
Juice from ½ lime

Rượu Martini Cốt Dừa

I don't see social drinking in Vietnam as much I did in the States, so to be offered a martini at a homestay is not very common. A martini glass alone is a rare sight. So when a homestay in the stunning mountains of Vietnam offers me a coconut cream martini, I will undoubtedly accept. I hope that every time you make this you can imagine yourself sipping on it while in the mountains of northern Vietnam overlooking the rice terraces!

1 For the coconut rims: Dip the rims of the chilled martini glasses into honey, and then coconut flakes for garnish, and set them aside.

2 For the martinis: Pour the coconut rum, vodka, coconut cream and fresh lime juice over ice in your shaker, and shake well.

3 Strain and pour into your chilled glasses.

The Pearl of Heaven

To you, the fields are beautiful—
Only that.
To me, they are food
To me, they are home
To me, they are kernel and soul.

To you, the fields are a picture to snap—
Only that.
To me, they are a battlefield
They are my history
They are my duty.

They offer their callouses
They offer their suffering
They offer their deaths—
Only if they could weep.

Instead, the rain falls
Sustaining them
Then breaks for singing birds.
Allow the songs to inspire you
To learn
To teach
To open your mind
As wide as the sweeping fields.

—PAUL B. KENNEDY

◀ **Mù Cang Chải**
rice terraces

Tracks and Traces

By now, you know a few things about me. You know that I am a traveler, not a tourist. *Traveler*, you might think, *he must have traveled his whole life...probably since he was in school, or, maybe right after.*

Well, no. It took me fifty years to get my first passport, so I definitely was not a born traveler. It wasn't a natural choice for me—I'm an introvert, and I'm in the habit of protecting my personal space.

But ever since I got my passport, I haven't stopped moving and exploring. I value that document—it opens worlds and perceptions, it provides air and light, it's the best kind of classroom—an engaging one. But how did it all begin?

As my fiftieth birthday approached, I found myself in a bit of a quandary. While most everyone I knew planned elaborate excursions for their fiftieth, I didn't understand why. I had never had the same wanderlust. I simply couldn't understand the appeal of going on vacations that seemed to offer little more than the chance to take a few selfies or snapshots of a pretty sunset. But even though I had reservations, I leapt onto the bandwagon and started to think about a trip.

◀ **A vendor selling fruit in Old Town, Hội An City**

Little did I know, this kernel of an idea would ultimately lead me around the world: across the ocean on my friends' yacht, to Rome, Greece, Turkey, Thailand, and ultimately, Vietnam.

As soon as I arrived in Hanoi, the capital of Vietnam, it felt like Kismet. I knew I had found my new home.

What sets Vietnam apart from other beautiful and ancient destinations? I was struck by the extraordinary warmth, kindness and generosity of the people. Here, the hospitality is unparalleled. I've been amazed over and over again by this community's resourcefulness, their compassion, and their willingness to help—even when it might not be convenient. People who don't know me well have asked me to join them for family dinners, invited me to their weddings, and asked me to celebrate the Lunar New Year or Tet with them. They've even welcomed me to come on vacations with them.

But I also fell head over heels in love with the city's culture, reflected in everything from the food, to the dress, to the language. What I initially thought was my idealized attachment to the vibe turned out to be a love and deep appreciation for both the people and the culture.

I discovered a vibrant place in Hanoi, a city rich in history and a unique juxtaposition of traditional and modern elements. Early on, I spent my days exploring many temples, museums and art galleries. I tasted countless new foods and drinks, each more delicious than the last. I traveled to the beaches, boated on the waters and motorbiked in the mountains.

Another way I immersed myself in the culture was to become an instructor in the city schools. Most often, I served as a volunteer. I taught local kids almost every subject—English, math, science and social studies. Because I got to speak to students daily, meet their families and engage with the faculty, I became familiar with local people faster than most newly arrived people do. On many days, my students were my coaches. They helped me answer questions, clarified cultural practices, and countered my misconceptions. Teaching gave me a sense of purpose but helped me contribute to a greater purpose, too.

I began to realize there's a difference between being content and being happy. For instance, in Hanoi, traffic jams are unavoidable and dramatic. When my friends and I find ourselves stuck on congested, gridlocked streets, we understand the situation and manage to be content with it. Happiness is another thing altogether. I'm convinced that when someone like me finds real happiness, it can be amplified by using one's experience to help others find their happiness too. And here, in Vietnam, I felt a sense of fulfillment that I had never experienced before.

◀ **Fisherman in Central Vietnam smoking the leaves of the *Nicotiana rustica* plant through a water pipe**
▶ **(Next page) Hội An sunset on the Thu Bồn River**

I hope this cookbook inspires you to learn more about Vietnam. I hope it encourages you, in a wide-ranging way, to open your heart to new places as you travel, to try new dishes, and to help you discover a place where you know you can be happy. Because that's the place where you belong.

Now, when friends visit Vietnam for the first time, I often encourage them to sample the same dish in multiple places as they travel throughout the country. This agenda is more interesting than it may sound. It's a way to experience a variety of tastes that reflect the wide regional variations in how people cook and eat. It's also a way to begin to understand how food evolves through history.

As you can see from my photos, rice flourishes here. And any table setting in Vietnam looks barren without a pair of chopsticks and a rice bowl. Rice is not only the essence of Vietnamese cuisine, but it's also central to the economy. You can't escape its presence—be it in the form of glutinous rice, rice noodles or rice papers. Often, it is a meal by itself in many households.

The entire culinary repertoire connects history to the tropical climate and the mountainous terrain. It's authentic and rich in other ways, too. Vietnamese cooking is seasonal. Locals enjoy bold, complex flavors. A transcendent spirit comes through with each savory bite, perhaps because the foods, like the people, all have stories to tell. Eating a celebratory holiday dinner is like listening to people reminisce whenever they are deeply sated and warmed by the closeness of a circle of friends.

I hope this book introduces you not only to recipes that are full or flavor and surprise, but that it also conveys some of the inspiration I've gained. Even more, I hope it in some way serves as a guide to finding your purpose and your happy place.

Tracks and Traces   **169**

Index

Acknowledgments

◀ A fisherman in Cao Bằng on a bamboo raft, wearing an *áo tơi* (traditional raincoat)

Wow, it finally got done! This book took much longer than I anticipated. It took a village, and I would like to express a big debt of gratitude to those who helped. I would like to thank everyone at Tuttle Publishing and Great Dog Literary. Special thanks to Jon Steever and Terri Jadick at Tuttle. At Great Dog, a special thanks to Liz Nealon and Mona Kanin. Between all of them they helped create the book that is in your hands. If you like the book, thank them.

To Dung Nguyen, just simply: thank you.

Thank you frequent flyer miles. Thank you affordable hotels and homestays. Thank you to my body for allowing me to sit on those little plastic chairs and still get back up without assistance.

This also goes out to anyone I didn't thank. Thank you for being you. Thank you even more for bothering to read the acknowledgments because I didn't think people read these.

Thank you everyone for making this book a reality.

"Books to Span the East and West"

Tuttle Publishing was founded in 1832 in the small New England town of Rutland, Vermont [USA]. Our core values remain as strong today as they were then—to publish best-in-class books which bring people together one page at a time. In 1948, we established a publishing outpost in Japan—and Tuttle is now a leader in publishing English-language books about the arts, languages and cultures of Asia. The world has become a much smaller place today and Asia's economic and cultural influence has grown. Yet the need for meaningful dialogue and information about this diverse region has never been greater. Over the past seven decades, Tuttle has published thousands of books on subjects ranging from martial arts and paper crafts to language learning and literature—and our talented authors, illustrators, designers and photographers have won many prestigious awards. We welcome you to explore the wealth of information available on Asia at www.tuttlepublishing.com.

Published by Tuttle Publishing, an imprint of Periplus Editions (HK) Ltd.

www.tuttlepublishing.com

Copyright © 2025 Paul B. Kennedy

ISBN: 978-0-8048-5741-3

28 27 26 25 24   10 9 8 7 6 5 4 3 2 1

Printed in China   2411EP

DISTRIBUTED BY

North America, Latin America & Europe
Tuttle Publishing
364 Innovation Drive
North Clarendon, VT 05759-9436 U.S.A.
Tel: (802) 773-8930
Fax: (802) 773-6993
info@tuttlepublishing.com
www.tuttlepublishing.com

Asia Pacific
Berkeley Books Pte. Ltd.
3 Kallang Sector, #04-01
Singapore 349278
Tel: (65) 6741-2178
Fax: (65) 6741-2179
inquiries@periplus.com.sg
www.tuttlepublishing.com

► **(Back endpaper) Breakfast with Vietnamese coffee and chocolate pancakes at a homestay overlooking the rice fields**